W9-DIG-604

Generalist Practice in Larger Settings: Knowledge and Skill Concepts

Also available from Lyceum Books, Inc.

Generalist Practice in Larger Settings: Knowledge and Skill Concepts

Thomas M. Meenaghan
New York University

W. Eugene Gibbons
Brigham Young University

LYCEUM
BOOKS, INC.

5758 S. Blackstone Ave.
Chicago, Illinois 60637

© Lyceum Books, Inc., 2000

Published by

LYCEUM BOOKS, INC.
5758 S. Blackstone Ave.
Chicago, Illinois 60637
773+643-1903 (Fax)
773+643-1902 (Phone)
lyceum@lyceumbooks.com
http://www.lyceumbooks.com

All rights reserved under International and Pan-American Copyright Conventions. No part of the publication may be reproduced, stored in a retrieval system, copied, or transmitted in any form or by any means without written permission from the publisher.

ISBN 0-925065-31-5

Library of Congress Cataloging-in-Publication Data

Meenaghan, Thomas M.
    Generalist practice in larger setting : knowledge and skill concepts / Thomas M.
    Meenaghan, W. Eugene Gibbons.
        p. cm.
    Includes bibliographical references and index.
    ISBN 0-925065-31-5 (alk. paper)
        1. Social service. 2. Social structure. 3. Social change. 4. Social service- -Case studies.
    I. Gibbons, W. Eugene, 1935– II. Title.
    HV41 .M389 2000
    361—dc21   00-021140

Dedicated to
Kathleen,
Christian, Mary, Peter,
and Rose
and
Evelyn,
Melody/Brian, Kurt/Linda, Denise,
Stephanie/John, Nathan/Debbie, Eric/Nikki,
and
Emily, Kristy, Jamie, Ashley; Megan, Jared, Amanda;
Lindsey, Rebecca, C. J.; Cameron, Jason, Tiffany;
Kassidi, Hunter; Tiani

CONTENTS

PREFACE

This book grew out of two sets of influences—the personal and the professional. On the personal side, the two authors first came to know each other when we both served on the Commission on Accreditation of the Council on Social Work Education. In the years we spent on the commission, and in the ensuing period, we each came to realize that while we were different in some ways, we shared a commitment to the importance of family and beliefs. Ultimately this personal compatibility led us to collaborate on this particular book.

On the professional side our collaboration was, in part, tied to a shared perception of how our profession's scholarship has been evolving over the past two decades. The literature has grown in terms of both quality and quantity. One of the specific areas that has grown quite extensively is the articulation of the generalist practice model. Central to this articulation has been the discussion of the problem solving model, as well as the need to appreciate the ecological perspective in practice. The latter strongly suggested to us that any book we developed should have a clear affinity for a range of social science theory and research.

However, when we looked closely at this growing body of literature, there were some discernable features that suggested which directions our book should follow. We came to the conclusion that although there was a substantial literature on generalist practice in small systems, there was not a corresponding body of literature stressing the requisite knowledge and skills needed to work in larger systems. Second, we felt that the excellent literature on practice in large systems that has dominated the field has not often been anchored in the generalist model. Rather, it has strongly stressed some advanced practice feature such as planning or administration, or it has done an outstanding job on some specific large system, typically organizations or communities.

Putting all these considerations together, we decided to write a particular kind of book—a book that would neither ambitiously attempt to achieve an overarching integrated social work theory nor stress the whole range of human behavior theory and knowledge, one that could relate to practice only in the broadest manner. Instead, we chose to build upon the literature of the generalist model, and to focus exclusively upon the selected knowledge and skills necessary to practice in larger systems. As such, we hope the book serves as a resource for the foundation curriculum and, in some instances, for those programs that have advanced generalist concentrations.

Because of its size and focus we do not see this book as being divorced from current practice or social science scholarship. Rather, we see its utility and strength in framing practice against the backdrop of a broad generalist framework and, within that framework, affording professors an opportunity to introduce their own thoughts and experiences. In fact, we encourage professors and students to enrich our material.

Finally, one additional thing is worth noting. As we wrote the book, each of us independently came to a conclusion that we share deeply. Generalist practice cannot be taught as a series of disparate skills and steps—rather, by nature, it has to be infused with knowledge which comes from practice and the social sciences. Because of this, we hope that in terms of curriculum areas the book is perceived as human behavior friendly; ideally, we sincerely hope it is seen as integrating practice and human behavior. It is our contention that when we as social workers feel comfortable and capable acting as macropractitioners, we are then empowered. As we utilize our knowledge and skills on behalf of our constituency—whether it be a neighborhood, a community, or an organization—they too have the potential to be empowered.

To return to the personal side again, we would like to thank those around us who helped make this book real. They include Kelsey Louie and Catherine Healey at New York University and Dr. Shirley Cox and Susannah Foster of Brigham Young University, who helped in numerous supportive ways. They also include our students and the graduates from our schools. Obviously, this enterprise, like all others that are significant, could not have been completed without the ongoing love and support of our wives and families. To them in particular, and to all who have helped, we give our heartfelt thanks and appreciation.

Finally, this is a shared product and the order of authors' names means nothing other than that there were two people involved in the writing and that they continue to really like each other now that the book is completed.

Peace,
Thomas M. Meenaghan
W. Eugene Gibbons

CHAPTER 1

Introduction and Overview

A lasting concern within the social work profession is the issue of practice scope—how specific or focused should anyone's practice be; or put another way, how broad or comprehensive should someone's practice be? This concern endures because it reflects at least two major considerations: 1) the possibility that specialization in practice does not imply true practice competency and 2) the idea that the organization of the external world requires practitioners to be able to make many kinds of practice interventions to help client systems.

This chapter, and the whole book for that matter, proceeds on the premises that practice with larger systems requires a definable set of skills and that all social workers should have a common understanding of how larger systems operate and how such systems might be engaged and even, at times, changed.

VALUE BASE AND PURPOSE

Over the past four or five decades awareness has grown that forces and processes in the larger social world influence people in a variety of ways (Popple & Leighninger, 1996). From what is called the "ecological perspective," people as individuals and as members of groups, organizations, and communities can benefit greatly from such forces and processes. When individuals interact with an external world that sustains and protects people, both the individuals and the groups to which they belong benefit.

Who would deny that when social processes geared to promoting education, public health, recreation, and related institutional supports function well, many people as a result develop as more productive human beings? Who would deny that when these processes work well, the groups and communities in which they occur may become even better groups and communities over time?

Within the ecological perspective is a twofold recognition: a) social forces outside the person can greatly influence the person in a positive manner (DiNitto & McNeece, 1997), and b) therefore, there is a normative, ethical obligation in the social world to make sure that processes and forces that work well are maintained.

In our complex world we cannot assume that positive social processes and forces will automatically be maintained. The fact of the matter is that competing demands on people's time and on that of organizations and communities are so strong that sometimes people only come to appreciate these processes and forces after their routine positive influence has broken down.

Generalist social work practice with larger systems assumes that social work intervention should be directed at 1) maintaining positive community social processes, 2) developing or restoring social processes that can contribute to human development and functioning, and 3) empowering individuals and small systems so that they will act to influence the larger systems affecting people's lives (Kirst-Ashman & Hull, 1997A). In short, intervention can focus on positive processes that facilitate prevention and furthering programs, or it can focus on restorative or empowering projects.

From the standpoint of values, several considerations are worth noting. First, people are entitled, as human beings, to a functional and positive community environment in which to act and grow. This entitlement, directly tied to the social nature of people, can in turn contribute to an evolving sense of social good and cohesion in the larger social world. In this regard, elements of both altruism and utilitarianism are potentially present when we reflect on community processes.

Derived from this value is a second professional value. It is necessary at times to intervene in the social world to maintain positive forces or redress damage done by negative forces.

Recognizing that social workers can and should focus on maintenance and remediation in the social world suggests a professional imperative. Effort and energy should be directed toward changing the external world. These changes would go beyond remediation. They might include basic, structural changes in roles, power, and prevailing social processes and begin to address the ends of social and economic justice. Examples in this area include efforts to change the relations and processes between whites and people of color, between gays and straights, and between those who are physically challenged and those who are not.

In short, an evolving sense of what is ethically right and fair has led to struggles, including social work interventions, to change basic relations and social processes between different groups. In this context, the value base for social work intervention in larger systems includes not just maintenance and remediation but also change and social justice.

In tracing the conscious pursuit of basic changes in the social world, the core values of social work are revisited and then operationalized in new ways. This is what the profession has always attempted. The core values include promoting the dignity of human beings, promoting people's right to develop to the fullest, and altering significant obstacles in the environment (DuBois & Miley, 1999).

In recent years, with the growth in literature and scholarship on the generalist practice model, concern about these values has been integrated with the problem-solving model. The problem-solving model in generalist practice at a minimum stresses study and assessment skills as prerequisites for designing and carrying out intervention plans. This book will emphasize how social workers can work with groups of people, organizations, and communities in a rational, problem-solving manner to maintain, restore, or even change selected processes, forces, and structures in the practice environment.

Chapter 2 discusses generalist practice as an organizing model of practice and introduces problem solving as an integrative practice framework. It also discusses the nature of social change and offers two specific models for facilitating change.

PRACTICE UNITS OF ATTENTION AS ACTORS AND TARGETS OF CHANGE

Generalist social work practice can emphasize such social units as organizations and communities as well as groups that may relate to or be part of organizations and communities. These social units may be seen as significant factors that impinge on people's functioning. At other times they may be seen as units at which some change-related activity can be directed. Whether the units are viewed as possible actors or as possible targets, the general purposes of intervention are the same: maintenance, remediation, change.

If we look at the same three social units as possible key *actors or subjects,* we can visualize the following examples in which the practitioner facilitates action on the part of the unit:

Organizations—Organizational initiatives directed at helping other organizations, groups, and communities to become more responsive to needs and risk in communities; helping other organizations to improve their programs and service delivery patterns; encouraging other organizations to maintain a broader range of service responses or to change or augment existing program responses.

Communities—Community initiatives directed at communicating with regional and state governments and economic powers and processes that operate both inside and outside of the community; dealing with key figures and organizations within the community that disproportionately influence the overall community's ability to develop and sustain processes that are functional to all members and groups in the community.

Groups—Informal, as well as formal, group initiatives directed at identifying organizations or institutional sectors that need to be developed, educated, or changed to ensure appropriate responses to the interests and needs of the group.

If we look at the same three social units as possible *targets or objects* of the practitioner's efforts, we can visualize the following examples in which the practitioner tries to effect change in the unit (Netting, Kettner, & McMurtry, 1998):

Organizations—Activities directed at making organizations more responsive to communities and groups; improving service delivery patterns; reinforcing efforts to continue programs that are seen as relevant or effective in a community; encouraging organizations to develop specific programs to meet unmet needs of individuals and groups.

Communities—Activities directed at promoting processes that develop or maintain peoples' involvement in the community; promoting key institutional sectors to address the needs of different groups in the community; developing and sustaining leadership and decision-making processes; changing aspects of community life that are dysfunctional or undeveloped.

Groups—Activities directed at promoting behaviors and processes in the smaller social worlds that make up the community, for example, kinship groups, networks, formal groups, and special interest groups.

This discussion suggests that there is both a conceptual and a real distinction between possible units of practice—organizations, communities, and groups—and how these units can be approached in generalist social work practice: as actors themselves or as targets of practice.

Practitioners need a working knowledge of the defining characteristics, theoretical considerations, and idiosyncrasies of both communities and organizations before attempting to enter or intervene with either unit. While the two units of practice have some commonalities because of their larger size, each possesses subtle and unique features. Chapters 3 and 4 spotlight a body of knowledge that can serve as a base on which the practitioner might build additional information and insights.

PRACTICE FRAMEWORK AND ROLE

Against the backdrop of the preceding material, it is useful to add two elements to our discussion, namely, framework and role. For the practitioner working in and with larger social units, it is useful to have a framework for making informed practice decisions and for engaging in self-directed practice responses.

In very general terms a practice framework has the following components: being critically attuned to the practice environment, acquiring relevant information, making judgements about problems and goals, selecting a change strategy, and then seeing if it works.

These logically related steps, viewed as a type of critical thinking, can be regarded as the problem-solving method applied to larger systems. They serve to guide worker thought, assessment, and practice behaviors. Further, they provide the general context within which the generalist practitioner identifies and selects from a broad range of role activities: serving as broker and linker among people, groups, and organizations in the community; educating and promoting awareness; initiating group formation; organizing and supporting groups; cultivating leadership; mobilizing resources; and planning political change. In chapter 2 we will specify how this general practice framework can be operationalized.

In focusing on certain role activities, the generalist practitioner must apply the practice framework to both rational and interpersonal or political aspects of situations. The rational aspect stresses the logical steps in problem solving, while the interpersonal or political stresses more subtle, though still significant, considerations tied to people, motivations, culture and traditions, interests, and power. Thus we have the marriage of science and art in social work practice.

It is essential that the practitioner understand that there is knowledge and theory that speaks to organizational and community behavior just as there is theory and knowledge that guides practice with individuals and small systems. Large systems cannot be understood simply be "enlarging" the values, norms, and dynamics associated with individuals and families. Trying to force microlevel theory onto macropractice is called "reductionism." Reductionist thinking assures failure when working with larger systems.

In order to facilitate understanding of the unique dynamics of practice with communities and organizations, chapters 5, 6, and 7 introduce a variety of skills, techniques, and strategies essential to successful macropractice. In all cases we will view the new material in light of the problem-solving practice framework established in chapter 2.

Finally, no discussion of social work practice is complete without attention to the evaluation of interventions employed by the practitioner. Chapters 8, 9, and 10 not only present the rationale and skills of program evaluation but also give an opportunity for the reader to evaluate her or his own understanding of the materials developed in the text, through the presentation of case materials. In chapter 10 the reader is encouraged to read each scenario in light of the new insights and knowledge gained from the text. The reader should pay special attention to the logical connections between chapters 8, 9, and 10 within the problem-solving practice framework.

CONCLUSION

In this brief introductory chapter we have attempted to identify the functional relations between individuals and processes involving larger social units. Selected social work values were identified and related to possible purposes of practice intervention with larger social units: maintenance, remediation, and change.

Organizations, communities, and groups are key social units that can become the focus of generalist practice. Such units can be dealt with as actors or as targets of practice interventions. In approaching such units a practitioner pursues varied role activities, but always within a general framework of problem solving. Rational thought and knowledge must always guide practice-related inferences and interventions; but rational thinking should be complemented by an appreciation of interpersonal and political considerations and an awareness that larger systems have their own structures and rules. Our focus on rational thinking leads logically to a discussion of practice evaluation. We now end this chapter with a charge to all practitioners: make the evaluation process an integral part of all practice planning, decision making, and implementation activities.

CHAPTER 2

The Generalist Model, Problem Solving, and Social Change

The previous chapter introduced the concept of practice in and with larger systems, explained why it is needed, and argued for its legitimacy. This chapter will focus on what a generalist practitioner is, how variable components of generalist practice are stressed, and what the relation is between generalist practice and critical thinking. Social change, and two specific modes of change, will be presented as a way to delineate how generalist practice can focus on work with larger systems. This emphasis on practice in larger systems will serve as a foundation for the specific body of knowledge and skills needed by generalist practitioners.

GENERALIST PRACTICE

Over the years several theorists have attempted to explicate the nature of generalist practice. For Johnson (1989) the generalist approach requires workers to recognize the different systems that interact with each other and with individuals. This interaction means that workers must appreciate the importance of specific systems before choosing a particular system at which to direct intervention efforts.

Kirst-Ashman and Hull (1997A) and Wells (1989) focus on the practice breadth and range of skills needed to facilitate interaction between people, situations, and social institutions. They conceive of generalist practice as the use of an eclectic knowledge base, infused with professional values, that supports a broad range of skills used to effect change in different size systems. Underpinning change efforts are such ideas as functioning and interaction, assessment, problem solving, critical thinking, and social justice.

As the field of social work has come to some level of consensus concerning the overall features of generalist practice, the need remains to distinguish between "generalist practice" and "generic practice." Generic practice refers to "universals," those elements "common" to all social work whether the practitioner is a generalist or a specialist in some specific method or pop-

ulation or even field of service (Anderson, 1982). Among the generic components of social work practice are the following: the task of matching needs and
resources; the functional role of the practitioner; the importance of a person-
in-environment framework; values such as acceptance, self-determination,
and individual dignity and self-worth; the importance of empowerment; and
the norms, values, and ethics of conduct captured in the profession's Code of
Ethics.

Recognizing the relation and distinction between the "generic" and the
"general," it might be said that generalists are those practitioners who, in light
of the generic base, are able to provide a vast array of services to client systems
of various sizes.

Years ago Pincus and Minahan (1973) identified the purposes of social
work practice: 1) to enhance the problem solving and coping capacities of
people; 2) to link people with systems that provide them with resources, services and opportunities; 3) to promote the effective and humane operation of
these systems; and 4) to contribute to the development and improvement of
social policy. From these basic purposes come the correlate practice imperatives. A focus on problem solving means that practitioners aim not just to
ameliorate problems but to teach critical life skills that will eventually
empower clients. A focus on linkage means that practitioners stress a person-
in-environment approach. Once the environment is appreciated, practitioners can assess interactions and transactions between different size client systems. By tying the person-in-environment approach to systems theory
practitioners can begin to shape organizing and integrating frameworks for
their practice. Practitioners in this way concentrate on negotiating a "fit"
between different systems.

Building on the purposes of social work practice discussed above,
Schatz, Jenkins, and Sheafor (2000) identify the four elements most distinctive of generalist practice:

1. A multidimensional, theoretical orientation that emphasizes the interre-
   latedness of human problems, life situations, and social conditions

2. A knowledge, value, and skill base that is transferable among diverse contexts, locations, and problems

3. An assessment method that is not constructed according to any particular
   theoretical or intervention approach (the generalist perspective requires
   the social worker to be eclectic—to draw ideas and techniques from many
   sources)

4. A selection of strategies and worker roles made primarily on the basis of
   an individual client's problems and goals and the sizes of the systems tar-
   geted for change

Throughout their discussion there is an appreciation not only of different size systems but of problem solving with different size systems. We will

now discuss each of these issues, and this will underpin the book's later treatment of knowledge and skills that are tied to problem-solving efforts appropriate to larger systems.

A WORKING MODEL OF PROBLEM SOLVING

Problem solving is now seen as an integrative practice framework. To understand how and why the generalist practice model has evolved as it has, we must recognize the overall influence of John Dewey on various aspects of problem solving and, as a result, on social work. Ultimately, social work has come to appreciate the utility of observing general patterns, reflecting on them, and then tailoring change efforts to special conditions and assumptions.

As social work has developed a normative ethical posture toward intervention in the world, the utility of well-defined, sequenced procedures has become apparent. The rational, goal-directed thinking and behavior that now characterize the profession stress structured connections among problem definition, gathering of information, testing, analysis of results, and revision based on test experiences.

This way of processing the phenomena found in different systems has specific applications in both social work research and social work practice. An early manifestation of rational thinking is exemplified in the following components of research cited by Selltiz, Jahoda, Deutsch, and Cook (1959): 1) a statement of purpose, that is, a formulation of the problem; 2) a description of the study design; 3) methods of data collection; 4) results obtained; and 5) conclusions and interpretations.

In social work practice, rational thinking is evident in the basic procedures in the prevailing practice framework: 1) problem identification and definition; 2) study, exploration, and data gathering; 3) differential assessment, planning, and intervention; 4) evaluation; 5) termination; and 6) follow-up. These are essentially the same steps as have been introduced in other practice methods. They draw heavily on the scientific method.

Most recently, social work has been greatly influenced by the concept of "critical thinking." This concept reinforces rationality and problem solving and has been applied to social work within the overall context of improving professional practice. Critical thinking involves the following:

> (1) a predisposition to question conclusions that concern client care and welfare; (2) asking "does it work?" and "how do you know?" when confronted with claims that a method helps clients, and also questioning generalizations about treatment methods and client; (3) weighing evidence for and against assertions in a logical, rational, systematic, data-based way; and (4) analyzing arguments to see what is being argued, spotting and explaining common fallacies in reasoning, and applying basic methodological principles of scientific reasoning. (Kirst-Ashman & Hull, 1997B)

Figure 1   Problem-Solving Worksheet

---

1. _**Study, Exploration, and Data Gathering**_

2. _**(Brief) Statement of the Problem**_

3. _**Assessment and Strategies**_

**Alternatives**	_**Hurdles**_	_**Consequences**_
a.	a.	a.
b.	b.	b.
c.	c.	c.
d.	d.	d.

4. _**Decision (Costs/Benefits/Feelings)**_

5. _**Implementation**_

  **a. Who**

  **b. When**

  **c. Where**

  **d. How**

6. _**Evaluation**_

  a. Did you implement your decision? Yes ____ No ____

  b. Did the anticipated consequnces occur? Yes ____ No ____

7. _**Follow-up**_

To make this discussion of problem solving concrete we introduce a problem-solving worksheet that can assist generalist social workers. Figure 1 is offered as an example of how a practitioner might approach a problem. In reviewing the worksheet, note some of the key concepts that have already been presented. The worksheet demonstrates the need to carefully identify the problem and to choose strategies linked directly to the problem. Note the influence of systems theory when alternative strategies are assessed. Although there is more than one way to reach a desired solution, some alternatives are too costly and the practitioner must understand this.

Perhaps one of the most difficult tasks facing a generalist practitioner is identifying, focusing, and succinctly stating the problem to be addressed. For example, in order to serve abused women, would a practitioner attempt to create a shelter capable of serving women and children, or only women? Would the shelter offer just housing and food, or would it provide clinical services? If basic clinical services were provided, would they be offered only to the women, or would children be served too?

In considering these questions, we begin to see why it is so critical to define the problem and needs accurately. The problem statement defines the scope, which, in turn, drives financing and staffing and determines the need for community support. As sufficient data is gathered, the problem begins to gain focus, the statement of the problem is properly articulated, and the practitioner can then look at strategies that might be used to address the problem.

The strategy planning step can quickly go awry if homework isn't properly accomplished. Strategies, if not carefully conceptualized, can complicate problematic situations. We often hear "Oh well! It can't get worse." Unfortunately, this isn't true, and in fact, poorly planned and executed strategies can backfire and cause serious problems. At times, ill-conceived strategies have "closed down"community services for years, even though those services were badly needed. For example, attempting to introduce a women's or children's shelter in a fairly conservative community without first understanding how residents feel about the role of family can be disastrous. Local citizens may jump to protect the "sanctity of the home." Their argument may be that the identified problems are actually personal matters that need to be handled by the family. Women's shelters *have* been successfully established in such communities, but success requires considerable homework and a carefully conceptualized plan of implementation.

In order to identify and choose from among alternative strategies a practitioner must possess a wide array of knowledge, skills, and techniques. The practitioner must have sufficient information and a clear enough vision of the problem to discern potential hurdles to the strategies being considered or developed. Some great ideas simply will not work because of built-in community resistance to the strategy being considered. It often requires analysis and sifting of information to know whether a given strategy is likely to succeed or is destined to fail. Desperately needed services can go by the board because the worker's tactics are not palatable to one or more constituencies in the community.

To move to another real practice situation, consider some of the nuances of the situation when a particular United Way agency board wants a specific individual named as executive director of a competing public agency. Suppose the executive director to be named will control a major funding source that is critical to the United Way agency—for example, the new director will determine who receives drug/alcohol passthrough funds from the state. Finally, suppose this is to be a political appointment made during an election year. What might the hurdles be to a chosen strategy? Would board members dare try to influence the political appointment? Would they make appeals to the candidates running for office, or would they perhaps try to influence the established governmental system? How visible would they make their own agency, or could they work through others in key community positions?

Many planners assume that a positive outcome will occur simply because a careful plan is employed. This assumption is just short of foolhardy. For example, imagine that the board chooses to support a political candidate who appears to be concerned about the issues and population associated with the United Way agency. Perhaps the board chose this candidate not only because of these interests but also because that candidate is strong and not easily intimidated. Unfortunately, these very attributes, which seem positive now, may well work against the agency after the candidate is elected. It is conceivable that the newly elected official might no longer be willing to hear or accept suggestions from the agency board once the election is won. Her stance may simply be that she already knows as much about the problem as the agency professionals do. Furthermore, the newly elected official may assume that agency personnel have a self-serving agenda that is antithetical to her constituency's best interests.

If practitioners use a faulty decision-making process, that process can become a hurdle in and of itself. When the group hasn't used good process, such as "group consensus," group members who feel invalidated or ignored might not work to accomplish the group's goals. For example, psych-techs in a community mental health facility may systematically delay the introduction of a new day treatment program if they haven't been involved in the development of the program from the beginning. There are a million little things they can do to delay the timing of the new project, and the delays can always be justified on the basis of what is best for the patient group at a given moment. The techs can show that the patients are too upset to move into something new, or that the unit is experiencing an AWOL (runaway) problem, or that they are still recovering from an attempted suicide. They have the ability to stop the project from moving forward, and they can do so seemingly on the basis of therapeutic considerations.

In addition to using sound problem-solving principles, effective practitioners must learn to elicit group members' feelings about the decisions that are finally reached. Practitioners will find that group members will still not move forward if their "feelings" or "gut" tell them that the process or end result will not be satisfactory. Good process includes attention to feelings and emotions as well as to carefully conducted problem solving.

However sound the group's proposed strategy is, ultimately the actual implementation is the key to success. Strange as it may seem, many groups develop good strategies that fail to move to implementation because there is no process in place to establish responsibility for followthrough. Action will not occur automatically. Indeed, some group members have no intention of being the ones to execute the group decision or plan. It is not uncommon for them to assume that the professional practitioner should carry out the "will" of the group. Another note of caution concerning implementation: some groups may appear to be paralyzed when it comes to moving their plan to the action stage. Implementation must be spelled out. Each group member should know who is responsible for each aspect of implementation, and how, where, and when should be clearly articulated.

But problem solving doesn't end with implementation. Without evaluation and follow-up on the plan, little can be learned from the experience. It is only as practitioners review the action plan and the implementation process systematically that invaluable learning takes place. There is no reason to step on the same land mine or reinvent the wheel again and again as each new project is undertaken. Social workers should learn with each experience and every project they work on. As they complete each project, practitioners should be able to see the universality of certain macrodynamics as well as those features unique to the project under review. Over time, practitioners learn how generalist practice and macrodynamics package themselves with the idiosyncrasies of the particular community or organization with which they are working. (Chapter 9 revisits problem solving.)

THE NATURE OF SOCIAL CHANGE

As the discussion has moved from the generalist model to an introduction of the problem-solving process and a problem-solving worksheet, it has become evident that work in larger systems requires distinctive knowledge and skills. Central to any practice with larger systems is a working understanding of social change and the strategies relevant to effecting change. This section will focus on the nature of social change.

Social change is a very complex and dynamic process. This is particularly true of change within large organizations and communities. While no one understands completely how and why change occurs, certain principles and theories seem to stand the test of time. For example, in talking about "the logic of collective action," Olson (1965) indicated that large organizations will only change for one of two reasons: because of incentives offered to the organization or because the organization is sufficiently coerced. An example of incentives occurred when the automobile makers of America were offered tax breaks for hiring people of color during the 1960s. In essence, the U.S. government made it worthwhile for the auto industry to be concerned about the critical civil rights issue of equal opportunity in employment. Coercion as a reason for change can also be understood within the context of governmental policy. The Occupational Safety and Health Administration and public health inspectors can bring considerable pressure to bear on organizations which must then modify conditions or incur hefty fines. It is interesting to watch large industries weight the costs of compliance against the costs of paying the fines levied against them. Coercion doesn't always work. It is often discouraging for young practitioners to learn that large systems seemingly refuse to do "the right things for the right reasons." It can be very disconcerting to hear organizations and institutions conclude that a cause is "just" and admirable but that they are not in a position to alter their organizational policies.

Robert Mayer (1972) suggests that "social change is related to the total social situation (social system) and its social structure." In social work, we constantly build on social systems theory. Systems theory helps us to understand interacting systems. When social workers talk about the way systems interact, invariably they are talking about the way systems organize and structure themselves. Mayer links three powerful concepts with structure: roles, status, and social relationships. He believes these are integral to an understanding of this larger construct. Simply put, *status* speaks to the position a person holds within a social system, prerogatives afforded the person by virtue of that position, and the value assigned to that position. *Role* is a dynamic concept and refers to the activities of a person within a social system. These activities obviously take place within a social context. Role is best understood in terms of assigned expectations and associated sanctions. All roles carry expectations as to the way a person should behave in *social relationships*. Sanctions are then applied in either a positive or a negative manner depending on the reactions of others to the person's role performance.

Another critical concept needed in order to understand social structure and social change is *stratification*. Acknowledging stratification is necessary for a clear understanding of democracy as it exists today. For example, Americans are told that all are born equal, but it is readily apparent that some are "more equal" than others. Max Weber (1947) in discussing stratification indicated that it can best be understood through three issues: *status* (prestige, esteem, reputation), *class* (economic), and *power*.

Two ways have been identified for acquiring status. First is what sociologists refer to as *ascribed* status. This is status with which a person is born and about which nothing can be done. Ascribed status cannot be obtained through upward mobility. Second is *achieved* status. This is status that reflects what a person is able to accomplish through personal effort (Parsons, 1964).

Society today is working to confer status less by ascription and more by achievement. Particular sensitivity has been shown recently to the status of women, gays and lesbian, and people of color. As might be expected, it is not easy to improve one's status in a culture of limited resources. There aren't many real-life Horatio Alger stories.

Instant wealth shows just how complicated stratification really is. For example, individuals and families who have won large sums of money in lotteries, though they have consequently moved up in class, are rarely accorded much status because their wealth may be viewed as fleeting or, even worse, undeserved. Many will remember the wonderful musical *The Unsinkable Molly Brown*. Molly is a classic example of how "old money" treats "new money."

Even though Molly owned half of Denver, she continued to be regarded as a "fly-by-night with poor ways."

Weber indicated that individuals might go up on one or two of the three elements he identified and down on another. For example, many professional athletes move up in income but make no upward movement in status or power. They may have money, but they continue to be viewed as "jocks" and as such are not invited to join the "power elites" who run the community. Many never finished their university educations and thus are not seen as viable leaders. They might well be treated as "new money" and viewed with considerable contempt (Giddons, 1984).

Another term is worth entertaining for just a moment—*life chances.* Much that goes into the American dream has to do with life chances. Basically, people lead their lives trying to attain life's valued goals and avoiding life's misfortunes. Life chances, then, refer to people's abilities to achieve valued goals and avoid misfortunes. Good life chances mean much more than wealth. They suggest the opportunities for education, improved employment, and ultimately better quality of life. Society tends to measure social success by examining income, education, and occupation. People often talk about income and occupation in their everyday discussions, with education being the means to achieve the other two.

When we discuss stratification together with life chances, we introduce the concept of *social mobility.* Social mobility means movement up and down the ladder of stratification. When social workers help people to improve their situations, they affect stratification. As people change, one of three things occurs: 1) everyone moves up the ladder, so stratification hasn't changed at all; 2) some people gain but no one loses (in order to accomplish movements of the first and second types society must come up with new resources, and many believe this to be impossible); and finally, 3) the whole stratification is reshaped so that some people gain and some lose. History suggests that people resist losing what they already have more than they worry about acquiring new assets. Many people oppose any attempt to change stratification because they believe only the third kind of change is possible. They worry when others acquire wealth because they are convinced that no *new* wealth is possible; it all must come from existing wealth, possibly their own.

In addressing stratification and mobility, we need to consider two additional concepts, *equality* and the *American dream.* The great American dream, very simply put, is that anybody, through hard work, can achieve and move from the "log cabin" to the "white house." The emphasis is on achievement and not on having position ascribed. The second concept, *equality,* is eagerly embraced but not systematically assured. In America, "equality before the law" and " equality of opportunity" are important concepts. These two imperatives have acquired even greater meaning since the civil rights movement of the 1960s; however, America still struggles with an even implementation of these societal values. Accepting the ideas of equality and the American dream does not mean making America a classless society; rather it means expecting all citizens to be assured the opportunity to improve their situations.

In the past three decades, an ideological effort has been under way in America to move from "equality of opportunity" to "equality of outcomes," where everyone is guaranteed certain benefits regardless of effort. This shift in philosophy has been criticized, however. The critics believe that by redistributing resources and income, it is possible to destroy or at least diminish what is often called the "work ethic." Moreover, they predict that an entitlement mentality that attempts to redress "relative deprivation" (in the eye of the beholder) rather than "actual deprivation" would create socialized medicine and other government-imposed programs that would ultimately cripple or destroy the country's free enterprise system. Finally, these critics fear that an entitlement-driven system will generate social conditions such as reverse discrimination. Already individuals have perceived themselves as having been denied access to law or medical school because of "quotas" or "preference" for diversity. Several legal verdicts suggest that entitlement mentalities actually serve to be discriminatory in their own way.

We now have a mosaic of interacting concepts and principles concerning social change. Let us turn our attention to some ways of altering social systems. Mayer (1972) postulates three primary means by which social systems are changed:

1. By reallocating the existing combination of roles and statuses to a different set of individuals or membership
2. By altering the combination of roles characteristic of a given structure
3. By redistributing the rights and obligations inherent in the statuses of the structure

Consider, for example, the evaluation of courses and instructors by students. Social changes occur when students in some systems are added to the evaluation process (*membership*); in other systems students create new *role* behavior or are afforded a new *status* that encourages them to become involved in evaluation. Social workers constantly find themselves involved with these three social change strategies as they attempt to advocate for the numerous populations in America at risk of discrimination.

THE RATIONAL MODEL AND THE FORCE FIELD PERSPECTIVE

We now present specific models of change that are related to generalist practice with larger systems. From among the many schools of thought on social change, we have chosen two conceptual models.

Rational Model

In our discussion of the scientific methods and critical thinking, we referred to rationality and logic. Finsterbusch and Motz have developed what is known as the *rational model* for policy decision making (Meenaghan & Kilty, 1993). Their model has five easily recognized and now familiar components:

> Specifying goals, identifying various options for achieving the goals, constructing criteria by which to evaluate action options, analyzing the advantages and disadvantages of each option relative to the criteria established, and selecting the option with the most advantages and the least disadvantage.

While acknowledging the many strengths of the rational model and rational thinking, Meenaghan and Kilty note some serious limitations associated with the use of the model that should be recognized. For example, practitioners don't always have the information needed to make reasoned decisions with this "idealized model." Many times it simply costs too much money to get the kind of data needed, and as a result, the information database is lacking. In this situation, it is difficult to arrive at a "reasoned" decision. At times, the decision making process becomes reactive rather than proactive. This often occurs as feelings taking precedence over logic. The rational model also ignores another very important reality of working with large groups. Often, competing groups and interests are involved in the decision making process, and many times their values are in conflict. These kinds of situations make for less than ideal decision making.

The rational model, though less than perfect, does require that the practitioner use the scientific method. Meenaghan, Kilty, and others identify the relevant principles associated with this model: 1) Reasoned judgment ties itself to evidence 2) Sound logic is essential to sound reasoning 3) The intent of rational and logical thinking is to be objective and to make a sincere attempt to be independent of what is studied 4) Orderliness allows focus on the material under study and sound methodology in the investigative process.

Since logic is such an integral part of rational thinking, perhaps we should take a moment to consider two quite different types of logic: deductive logic and inductive logic. *Deductive logic* from *general* principles and conclusions to a *particular case or situation* (or from "the whole" to "its parts"). It's a movement from the *universal* to the *individual*. Deductive logic is an analytical exercise. In essence, a conclusion is drawn concerning a particular situation predicated on a larger, more general principle. The following statement is an excellent example of deductive logic: "All individuals with incomes below $5,153 fall below the poverty line. Paul's income is $5,434. Therefore, Paul does not fall below the poverty line" (Meenaghan & Kilty, 1993).

Inductive logic synthesizes, organizes, and combines facts. It is a movement from parts to the whole, or from the *specific* to the *general*. An example of inductive logic can be found in a student graduate school reference letter where the faculty member concludes that a student will perform well in an MSW program because he performed well in many related undergraduate classes. Central to inductive logic is evidence on which to base conclusions. This process leads to verification of findings and, invariably, to further study or research.

In sum, deductive logic stresses the value of generalized explanation—typically referred to as theory—inductive logic stresses the value of evidence. Both theory and evidence are essential to the scientific method.

The rational model is process driven and requires practitioners to approach problems rigorously and systematically. It demands clarity about the type of logic being used, and it relies heavily on the cognitive attributes of the practitioner.

Force Field Perspective

Kurt Lewin (1952), the father of the force field perspective, suggested looking at possible barriers to the achievement of given goals as a way to understand the factors that can lead to success.

Before proceeding, it is important that we introduce concepts that will facilitate understanding of Lewin's contribution to generalist practice. Lewin sought to explain the dynamics experienced when practitioners interact with groups. By suggesting that a group is more than, or more exactly different than, the sum of the members who come together for a particular project, he viewed a group as a gestalt, or as an integration of its members as contrasted to a summation of its members. This notion suggests that a group possesses its own structure, its own goals, and its own relations to other groups. According to Lewin, each group possesses and experiences a *need* that is linked to unfulfilled group goals and this need produces a *tension*, which becomes the energy that group members draw on to fulfill the unmet need. Thus group tension can only be alleviated by accomplishing group goals. Lewin insisted that groups are committed to the reduction of tension and a return to equilibrium.

Before moving to the force field perspective, one other concept that is critical to understanding Lewin needs to be presented. This concept has to do with what Lewin calls *life space* (Hull, 1971). A person's life space is the environment as she or he views (perceives) it and as the life space in turn affects the viewer's behavior. We are not suggesting that every group member's perception of a particular event is accurate. We are simply saying that each group member will act upon his or her perception as if it is accurate. Group members thus come together in a shared group life experience that can be very interesting. Lewin's perspective helps practitioners to understand how and why certain group members function the way they do in groups. It clearly helps to explain certain small group dynamics. These few concepts can also assist practitioners in their understanding of Lewin's force field model.

When discussing force field analysis, Kirst-Ashman and Hull (1997B) suggest that typical barriers or constraints facing a practitioner involve lack of resources such as money, people, laws, rules, and so forth. Brueggemann (1996) calls the barriers "restraining forces"; these are the disadvantages and costs associated with the solution under consideration. (Recall that the problem-solving worksheet earlier in this chapter introduced the concept of barriers, or hurdles.) He calls "driving forces" the advantages or benefits of the solution being considered. Brueggemann further suggests that time, money, manpower, quantity, quality, and effectiveness are the variables needed to assess and compare the various solutions available.

Figure 2 shows Brueggemann's schematic tool for evaluating the relative strengths of the restraining and driving forces associated with a particular proposed solution.

This section of the chapter will close with a five-step procedure that practitioners can use to analyze a given problem from the force field perspective. The steps are elaborated briefly through a hypothetical practice situation.

1. *Specify the desired change or objective*—Develop respite services and support systems for those in your community with AIDS.

2. *Identify the driving and restraining forces that must be considered to assure success of your desired objective*—Identify the groups (parents or friends), agencies, hospitals, professional organizations, religious organizations, and the like, that will assist you in your endeavors. These are the driving forces and are defined positively. Next, identify the organized groups of individuals or decision makers who will vehemently oppose helping the identified population. These are the restraining forces.

3. *Assess the strength of the driving and restraining forces*—In assessing these forces, consider the impact of the following three concepts: potency, consistency, and amenability. *Potency* simply means the strength or power of a particular force (Lewin called this *valence*). Is the support for AIDS respite care really going to come forward and be counted? On the flip side, how strong is the resistance to the project? Are detractors really determined to block your efforts? The second concept, *consistency,* means the stability of the position taken. Will supporting individuals and other coalitions stand solidly behind the respite effort, or will they fade when things get rough and tension escalates? Is the opposition apt to weaken over the long haul? *Amenability* means the openness of a particular force to outside influence and pressure. Are the opponents of respite care amenable to education and reason, or are they going to be driven by emotion and perhaps even hysteria?

4. *Identify the actors*—The actors are persons, groups, or organizations that might be called on to influence the forces, thus altering their strength.

Figure 2   Force Field Analysis

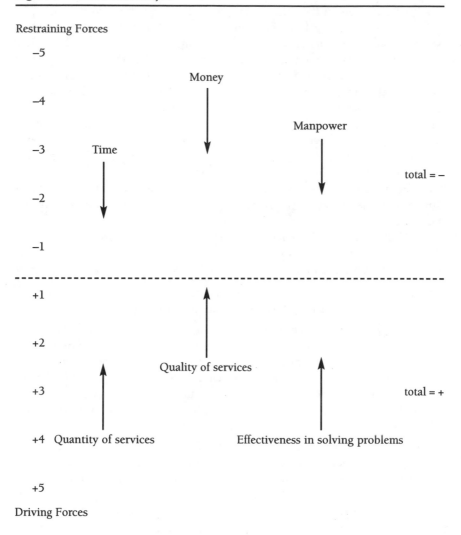

Restraining Forces

−5

Money

−4

Manpower

−3   Time

total = −

−2

−1

- -

+1

+2

Quality of services

+3   total = +

+4   Quantity of services   Effectiveness in solving problems

+5

Driving Forces

The key forces are the church, community, and professional leaders who will speak in favor of respite care, as opposed to the influential people who will attack the concept on moral grounds.

5. *Select a strategy for change*—After completing the four steps above, list each component force (dynamic) on a scale of high to low. Now consider the information and identify a strategy that will ultimately strengthen the driving forces and weaken or invalidate the restraining forces. The whole point of this exercise is to determine the strength of a position as compared to the strength of the opposition. Strategies can then be matched

to the elements in force. Remember, strategies can never be the same from one project to another. (Sheafor, Horejsi, & Horejsi, 2000)

THE ROLE OF POLITICS IN MACROPRACTICE

Social workers often say that they are not political and that they have no desire to become involved in political activity or any form of social action. They don't want to dirty themselves in a process they disdain. Some practitioners find the political process too conflictual, too emotionally draining, and too unfulfilling. Moreover, it's a process they can't control, so the nature of the activity increases their anxiety and stress. Admittedly, politics is often unpredictable enough to make some practitioners feel very uncomfortable. Unfortunately, however, there is really no such thing as a successful, competent, and effective *nonpolitical* social worker. By virtue of professional ethics, values, and training, social workers are committed to social change, and this commitment puts the generalist practitioner right in the middle of the political process. Perhaps the term "politics" is too strongly associated only with those involved with public office or the legislative process. In fact, it means something broader: to be political is also to understand political influence and political activity, to recognize "power brokers," "string pullers," and "movers and shakers," and to appreciate other delicate relations within agencies and communities. Polsby's (1963) discussion of politics is most relevant to generalist practice in larger systems. Polsby defines politics as "the recognition of, and subsequent action by, groups and individuals of their interests that are directly tied to their positions in social relationships" (quoted in Meenaghan & Kilty, 1993).

This definition has widespread ramifications. Polsby clearly states that when people come together for purposes of social change, they do so out of self-interest and are motivated by their personal attitudes and values. Polsby also stresses the concept of stratification, raised earlier in this chapter. He suggests that power, status, and role are critical aspects of the political arena. Generally speaking, even well-intentioned people and groups cannot routinely overcome actors or forces that possess power and position.

Practitioners need to know and understand the actors with whom they are involved, and they need to know about formal and informal power. Extensive knowledge about and experience with social relations is also essential to success in practice. When dealing with "politicals," social workers are not always dealing with purely rational and objective individuals. "Politicals" will not always be inclined to "do the right things for the right reasons." Many times they may smile and nod their heads in agreement with the presentation being made and yet vote against the proposal later in the meeting.

It is not easy for people to give up points of view to which they are attached emotionally and psychologically. It's like moving from being right to being wrong! Change is difficult for most people, and many will resist it in an attempt to maintain their equilibrium. So in the political world, resistance is more often than not the norm. Resistance has its own energy and the practitioner's work is often to process and reform the resistance and its energy to bring about change. We will devote further discussion to this topic later.

While political effectiveness in generalist practice is to be encouraged, there are nevertheless possible traps associated with being politically effective. Rapp and Poertner (1992) suggest some of the problems with political effectiveness:

> Failure to recognize that the demands made by the external constituencies are often unsupportive of or incompatible with or irrelevant to client well-being. In our quest for survival or positive opinion by elites (Perrow, 1978), we may waste precious time that could be better spent helping clients, or more importantly, we could be unwittingly join[ing] a coalition that will harm clients.

Rapp and Poertner give the example of a child protective service worker spending too much time trying to please the police, district attorney, or judge at the expense of the parents and child. All of a sudden, protecting the child and protecting the rights of the parents becomes lost in pleasing other key actors or constituencies.

Bennis, Benne, and Chin (1969) also warn of possible difficulties associated with institutional change:

> Change agents [may overestimate] the capability of political action to effect changes in practice. . . . Change agents who have worked hard for the law, ruling or decision frequently assume that the desired change has been made. Actually all that has been done is to bring the force of legitimacy behind some envisioned change.

These authors very clearly warn that practitioners need to work with the affected people in a reeducation effort. A change in law or policy can bring about new attitudes, new values, and a need for new knowledge and skills. Change can often be quite traumatic to its constituency, and this change requires corresponding adjustments in the norms, roles, relations, and structures of organizations and institutions. Without such follow-up, the implementations of change can go in directions not really intended.

CONCLUSION

In this chapter we reviewed the concept of generalist practice as it relates to practice with different size systems. We identified the relation between generalist practice and generic social work, as well as the differences between the two. We presented the integrative framework of rational problem solving, and it served as a precursor to the topics of social change and possible models for effecting social change. These latter topics strongly suggest that distinctive knowledge and skills are necessary in practice with larger systems. Finally, the chapter closed with a brief discussion of the political aspects of macropractice.

CHAPTER 3

Working with Organizations

Practitioners working in larger systems typically carry out their activities as members of an agency, hospital, or community organization. Since practitioners are rarely if ever freestanding, discrete actors, it is important to visualize generalist practice as heavily shaped by organizational realities, organizational dynamics and processes, and the needs and purposes of specific organizations.

Practice can be shaped in two major directions (Meenaghan & Kilty, 1993). First, the practitioner as a potential actor can be tightly constrained by existing organizational rules and guidelines. For example, a practitioner may think that counseling should be integrated with a particular benefit. Yet if the organization provides only one or the other of the services, the practitioner is constrained by existing service decisions operating within the organization. Consider major comprehensive mental health centers. They simply do not offer services to the majority of the community. Many of these centers are restricted to serving the chronically mentally ill and are not available to those needing general psychiatric services.

Conversely, another organization may refuse to extend a particular benefit to a client unless the client actively engages in other services simultaneously, such as counseling or peer support. For example, many private residential schools for children and teenagers who are disturbed or acting out will not take a child unless the parents are willing to be actively involved in the interventive and educational process. This is true even when the child is placed in another state. Ongoing communication is thus required through telephone calls, written correspondence, occasional parent visits, and prearranged and monitored child home visits. In such instances the organization's expectation is also a constraint on a member practitioner, but with the opposite result.

Second, organizations can be committed to certain goals that encourage practitioners to expand existing service responses. For example, an organization may have a very clear commitment to advocating on behalf of the developmentally disabled and their families. Within this organizational context, practitioners, individually or collectively, might find themselves initiating practice responses that are unusual or unexpected by the organization. Seeking out legal resources or organizing affected parents, while not "normal" procedure, might nevertheless be quite in keeping with the organization's overall purpose. In this case, the organization, because of its stated mission, actually stretches practitioners, prompting them to think beyond existing service responses (Gates, 1980). Many state mental hospitals and mental health centers, for example, actively encourage the parents of their clients to become involved with NAMI, a family support organization with a strong educational and social action agenda.

Organizations can also be viewed as targets requiring change-related activity (Kirst-Ashman & Hull, 1997A). Let's return to the example of an organization that mandates a separation of benefits from counseling. Member practitioners, through their own experience and research and the research of others, may conclude that such a separation is dysfunctional for the client group or for the organization itself. In this situation, the practitioners might well consider examining why and how the organization came to this position.

Similarly, practitioners in the wider community may encounter this organization's requirement that benefits and counseling be separated. These community-based practitioners may come to the same tentative judgment that the separation is dysfunctional. Therefore, practitioners working in other organizations may feel it is necessary to try to educate the organization about the advantages of integrating benefits and counseling, or to at least enter into discussions about new ways to better serve clients—especially in terms of such program questions as why, how, for how long, and so on.

Examples of services or benefits being available but without supportive counseling can be observed in the many states trying to enact the new federally mandated welfare reform. States are in the process of reducing the number of people receiving financial assistance and are committed to terminating clients from welfare rolls within three years, but in many instances no effective counseling programs are in place to assist clients in realistic attempts to get "off" welfare.

To both sets of practitioners—within and outside—the organization is a possible target for change, or at least a party that might want to examine its current position that certain services and benefits should be separate.

Practitioners in organizations, therefore, must understand clearly that they always practice as extensions of organizational decisions and that they will often confront such decisions, whether of their own or another organization (Kirst-Ashman & Hull, 1997A). This being the case, practitioners must understand the nature of organizations—their characteristics, dynamics, and cultures—to know when such factors can be used to promote change and when such factors should be viewed as possible targets of change on behalf of client groups.

AGENCIES AS COMPLEX, FORMAL ORGANIZATIONS

Agencies in communities can be described in part as rational, thought-out mechanisms that exist to achieve certain ends (Netting, Kettner, & McMurtry, 1998). In the social service world, agencies are specific devices created in different community settings to assist people and groups in a variety of ways—to protect children, to provide families with needed support, to develop appropriate or necessary benefits for the elderly, and so on. Different people have figured out what services certain types of people need and what specific helping groups can or should offer; as a result a variety of programs have become routinized.

As appropriate responses became clearer, and as they were delivered over and over, one central question came to the forefront: How do we organize our professional workers and support workers, in short, our human resources, to best serve the people we wish to serve—to best meet their needs? The response to this question is reflected in all aspects of life—in social services and elsewhere: a formal organizational model.

Formal organizational structure is a conscious attempt to rationally arrange and interrelate human workers, who vary in skills, training, and competencies, to achieve collectively what the organization says it wishes to achieve. In the world of social services, this generally means helping some group of people to meet certain needs or reach certain goals (Miringoff, 1980). Not all ways workers can be put together are equally valued, however. Organizational structure is typically guided by two principles: *coverage* and *efficiency*—that is, serving everyone at the lowest cost consistent with high quality.

Many classical theorists, Weber, Scott, and Blau, among others, have specified characteristics that organizations as formal and rational bodies should have if they are to use varying human resources efficiently (Blau & Meyer, 1971). These include specialization of roles, coordination of roles, uniform rules and procedures, rewards and sanctions tied to rules; and personal disinterestedness (Meenaghan, Washington, & Ryan, 1982).

The foremost characteristic of formal organizations is *specialization*. Basically, specialization exploits the variation among different people in skills, education, and training. By having people do what they're best able to do, and almost only that, the organization addresses its purposes and goals as efficiently as possible. Specialization has two predictable consequences: First, specific roles and tasks become much narrower than what any worker is potentially capable of doing—put another way, given role behavior is much smaller than human potential. Second, the very narrowness of the role behavior encourages repetitive behavior, and that repetition can increase the efficiency and proficiency of the worker in the given role.

There is a principle associated with specialization often invoked by professional social workers. It's called the "Peter principle." Because specialization tries to fit a worker's role to his or her particular strengths, the worker may appear to be more generally skilled than is in fact the case. The worker may thus be promoted to a new position that is not necessarily as suited to his or her skills because administrators overlook the contribution that specialization has made to the worker's performance. Should the worker succeed in this new position, he or she may well be promoted again. Indeed, the Peter principle asserts that a practitioner will be promoted until he or she reaches a "level of incompetence." The principle is easy to understand, but it is difficult to manage. Social work is notorious for placing unprepared and untrained practitioners in positions requiring specialized knowledge and skill. Remember, being a well-trained generalist practitioner does not guarantee competence as a supervisor or administrator (Peter & Hull, 1994).

Once an organization assigns its workforce to a series of different work roles, the different roles obviously have to be *coordinated.* Ideally, such coordination involves both horizontal and vertical linkage. Horizontal linkage involves relations among organizational equals. It exists, for example, when intake workers relate to case planning workers, who in turn relate to intervention specialists. Such linkage can occur among programs too—for example, when inpatient programs relate to aftercare or daycare programs. Vertical linkage involves relations between colleagues of unequal status and responsibility in which one worker has authority over the other. Vertical linkage invariably implies unevenness of power and authority. It exists when several intake workers relate to a common supervisor and when several aftercare workers relate to their own common supervisor. Both supervisors in turn relate to each other (horizontal linkage) and are accountable to, say, an associate director of services (vertical linkage).

Activities such as coordination, supervision, and interrelating of people and roles clearly define a unique role—that of manager and administrator. A hallmark of all organizations is not just specialization, but this linkage and coordination among different, specialized units and workers.

A third characteristic that organizations rely on is *uniform rules and procedures* (codified in policy and procedures manuals). These procedures are important because they represent the standard or best way for workers to do their jobs. They guide worker behavior and eliminate the need for each worker to stop and create new answers for each situation. In this way uniformity, speed, and efficiency are all achieved. In an ideal organization these procedures are the evolved, "wisest" ways to operate. These procedures also become a major ingredient in managers' evaluation of workers. Managers can ask, Does the staff member routinely reflect in his behavior what the organization expects? Managers, in light of the rules, can judge workers as meriting *rewards* or requiring negative *sanctions.* Thus we see a link between the concept of rules and procedures and "role theory." Role theory suggests that individuals act in relation to understood expectations and sanctions linked to the roles they fill.

Even with a suitable reward structure, staff in organizations will have a difficult time adhering to organizational rules and procedures without a certain amount of *personal disinterestedness*. Staff cannot become too involved in the unique aspects of their work, especially with other people, including clients. The reason for this is that strong, personal involvement with the unique features of the job and of clients might make it too difficult to apply uniform procedures. When this occurs, speed and efficiency can suffer, and fewer people can be served. In short, the organization wants the practitioner to maintain appropriate professional distance. The implicit suggestion is that workers who become too familiar with their clients and cross "client practitioner boundaries" will overidentify with the clients against the organization.

The five characteristics we have discussed help a complex organization to be an enduring, rational social structure. However, they also suggest some of the predictable problems or dysfunctions often present in complex organizations.

First, commitment to following rules may produce not just an enduring, rational, predictable social structure but, indeed, a static, ritual-prone organization incapable of changing to meet new situations. Sometimes this is called organizational *inertia*. Inertia is often viewed by the practitioner as "rigidity." Day-to-day activity in an organization suffering from inertia is devoted to meeting the letter rather than the spirit of the law. This clearly suggests that the social structure of the organization and its subsequent policy does not conduce to meeting the needs of the clients served.

Such inertia is not surprising in light of the way communication may become constrained in some organizations. If rewards and sanctions are too rigidly tied to rules and procedures, staff will pass only limited controversial information up the vertical hierarchy. The information that is suppressed may relate to staff performance—for example, it may be about situations that staff members may not have handled well because they were new, or the situations were intrinsically thorny, or existing procedures did not really apply. The result is that supervisors and managers do not routinely receive potentially very significant information.

If there is *blockage in vertical communication,* key decision makers have only part of the information they need in order to make sound organizational decisions. The rational nature of the organization is thus threatened, and the organization's ability to remain relevant can be compromised. Information blockage can easily occur in a governor's or senator's office if the staff is "laundering," filtering, or managing the information going to the elected official. This often happens when staff members operate from their own agenda or assume that they understand the position the elected official holds when in fact they don't. Managers and administrators may also lack relevant knowledge because specialization insulates them and limits their experiences.

Specialization carries other dangers as well. When there is not adequate managerial coordination, *fracturing* may occur among related roles and work units. Such fracturing makes rationality and efficiency much more difficult to achieve.

Finally, when staff operate in a work environment that emphasizes repetition and the dominance of procedures and managers, they may begin to find the work boring and the conditions of work alienating. *Alienation* is a social-structure-induced social psychological condition. It predictably arises in overly controlled work environments that do not respect broad individual variations, especially those related to creativity. Staff members who become alienated—who "burn out"—show a variety of responses: minimal compliance, organizational deviance, excessive passivity, dislike of work or fellow workers, and even dislike of clients. Obviously, alienation does not conduce to efficiency or rationality within the organization. When too many practitioners burn out, the organization becomes even more static and unresponsive to clients and to whatever correction is needed.

MORE RECENT WAYS TO LOOK AT ORGANIZATIONS

Many people, in a wide variety of settings, have come to see organizations not as rational and efficient structures but as somewhat irrational and inefficient structures that are at times quite flawed in their ability to achieve their goals. We will talk about two ways organizations can attempt to compensate for the possible dysfunctions cited about—dysfunctions that are tied to organizations' very differentiated and stratified structures of roles and statuses.

The first approach stresses using staff competencies in very specific ways to address specific, changing goals (Fisher & Karger, 1997; Netting, Kettner, & McMurtry, 1998). This perspective recognizes that the existing structure already assigns workers to particular roles but asks the question, Given the existing staff, who has the skills needed to get a specific project completed? It also goes further and raises the possibility that the person assigned to lead a project need not always be a major person in the organization.

In short, this strategy says that while organizational structures are important, certain projects can be better addressed by culling the most competent and assigning leadership responsibility for the specific project to someone who has demonstrated the skills needed to bring the project to completion. This approach suggests that reliance on the vertical and status properties of an organization must be tempered by an appreciation that specific competencies should fit specific projects.

Another approach is the systems approach. It stresses the need to see organizations as having external environments as well as internal processes (Meenaghan & Kilty, 1993; Thompson, 1967). This approach to organizations posits that organizations through time structure their resources, which include their workers, into programs to produce some desired outcomes. This being the case, an organization wants to know whether its use of resources is indeed producing these outcomes. If it is not, because of the characteristics of rationality and efficiency the organization must structure its resources differently. It would be irrational to keep doing the same things in the same way if they aren't producing the intended result. Once a new structuring of resources is in place, this changed use of resources is also monitored and evaluated.

Besides the important consideration of whether the desired effect is being produced, an organization wants to know whether conditions in the external environment continue to warrant its specific use of resources. If an organization is witnessing real changes in the populations or problems in its environment, it has to raise questions of relevancy: Is the organization's structured use of resources related to what the current population in an area needs? Does the organization's structured use of resources relate well to "new" or emerging problems? If the answers to these questions are no, the organization must fit itself to the new conditions in its environment. Again, once the new structured use of resources is in place, it is monitored and evaluated relative to the effects desired.

In addition to changes in the populations or problems facing an organization, there may be significant changes in other key areas. For example, funding sources or the concerns of funders may change. At one point, an external funding source may make financial resources available to address the needs of battered women or issues of mental health. Over time, however, political and legislative initiatives may move priorities away from these areas toward family preservation and correction. Organizations that rely on particular funding sources have to deal with these kinds of funding changes or face the possibility that they might not have the financial resources needed to deliver structured responses. This eventuality is evident with the annual funding cycle of the United Way. While there is a degree of stability in its funding schedules, it is nonetheless mandated to address current issues, and there are rarely significant increases in contributions from year to year. Consequently, when funding shifts toward an organization addressing what the United Way regards as important issues, there will be less for other agencies.

Similarly, sentiment and expectations in the community might change over time. Communities can become more understanding and supportive of certain kinds of initiatives by organizations; they might also become less understanding and supportive. Obviously, it is in the interests of an organization to be familiar with current community attitudes and with trends in these attitudes.

Against the backdrop of the systems perspective, certain basic ideas need to be summarized. Organizations must realize that however they choose to structure their use of resources, use should be subject to desired outcomes being produced, tied to external environments and possible changes in populations and problems, and tied to community expectations and funder realities. If organizations follow these principles, they can claim that they are not just rational and efficient but also effective, relevant, and capable of meeting the expectations of key constituencies. Of course, for organizations to operate fully in line with these principles, they must have a commitment to change when necessary and to regular inquiry about their internal processes and external environment.

SOME PROBLEMS IN HUMAN SERVICE ORGANIZATIONS

In the preceding discussion we made reference to possible problems in organizations: inertia, limited information, fracturing of specialized units, and staff alienation. These problems exist in many human service organizations, contributing to and reflecting basic dysfunctions in the structure of these organizations.

Human service organizations must be alert to potential problems in some specific areas (Meenaghan & Kilty, 1993):

Access—The types of people who come to the organization may not be fully representative of the community profile or the organization's purpose. Typically this involves considerations of age, gender, race, family structure, social class, and sexual orientation. Some groups might be greatly overrepresented or underrepresented. Moreover, some people will not avail themselves of public services. They always look to the private sector for help. Many seem to have concluded that good practitioners will not work for the county, state, or federal government.

Utilization—While many types of people routinely come for service, certain specific subsets of people may be routinely sent or referred elsewhere. Organizational purpose or availability of other organizations *might* explain the routine referral pattern—but it might not.

Coordination/duplication—A few, or even many, organizations may offer similar or identical services to the same populations. In extreme cases, this overlap produces competition among the human service organizations and contributes to irrational and inefficient use of resources. It is also associated with an inability to identify unmet needs that could be addressed with existing resources. When organizations focus excessively on duplicative services, they are unlikely to be scanning their environments for unmet needs, changing needs, and so on.

Decision base and decision structure—The amount and type of data available for rational decisions may be limited, as may the involvement of potential key actors in making organizational decisions. Many human service organizations collect lots of information about clients, but they do not necessarily use this information in making ongoing organizational decisions. Usage patterns can be tied to what information is systematically collected, how it is stored, and how it is accessed. For example, information on social class (education, income, or occupational type) is often not stored accurately or reliably. Yet this information when looked at collectively could help an organization to determine whether to maintain or change some of its dealings with the community. Further, information stored in case records might not all be stored in computer-accessible formats as well. In this situation, decisions based on analysis of the organization's database will not necessarily be tied to actual configurations of data in case records.

Besides having an inadequate information base from which to make decisions, an organization may have an incomplete decision structure. As remarked earlier, vertical hierarchy and rule-based sanctions can together create an environment in which only limited and biased information is available to decision makers. This propensity combined with the typical structural and even physical separation between decision makers and the daily activities of the organization places decision makers in the peculiar position of having disproportionate power and limited information. In this situation, it may be hard to achieve routine, predictable, rational decisions at the organizational pattern.

Program contingencies and ongoing planning processes—Ideally, several representative areas of the organization routinely look at how operations relate to desired outcomes; similarly, some type of planning body within the organization reflects on and ultimately chooses desired outcomes. In both instances, some formalized review or evaluation process is useful, and the need to create alternative, contingency plans is clear. However, some organizations don't have either in place and are more prone to do "something" when a crisis arises. Such a reactive mode clearly implies limited rationality and inefficiency; it also suggests little if any commitment to preventing problems and to undertaking timely systems analysis and change. This tendency in organizations is often a result of incomplete information and decision arrangements.

Intraorganizational staff relations—In the social work arena, largely because of the influence of personality theory, interpersonal work tensions and conflicts are often assessed as individual problems. In some cases this assessment may be correct, but typically some aspect of the organization itself is contributing greatly to the situation. Sometimes workers or different units within an organization engage in serious conflict simply because of ambiguity about how certain roles, with their rights and responsibilities, should perform. Workers often don't know the extent to which they are free to make independent decisions without first clearing them with their superiors. If they feel they must clear all decisions, they may well complain of being micromanaged; and morale will suffer. Lack of agreement tied to lack of clarity encourages actors to assert their own interpretations, and this can produce conflict. This kind of conflict can be addressed by clarity in work description.

In other instances, clarity may be present, but staff disagree fundamentally about why occupants of certain roles are afforded the rights and responsibilities they are. This is a different kind of staff conflict, and it requires negotiation.

Most basic of all is conflict between workers about performance. Some workers, in the eyes of other workers, just don't perform well, and their failings have a negative impact on others, even on organizational outcomes. This kind of conflict requires staff training, and if that fails, staff replacement.

THE ROLE OF ORGANIZATIONAL CULTURE

The concept of culture—though often associated with large groups of people—in some instances, with whole countries or regions—simply means shared or prevailing values and norms that guide the behavior of members of a group and that provide a context and perspective for their aspirations and expectations. Culture, as an idea, can thus be applied to very small systems—families, groups, and organizations.

Organizations, including those in the human service arena, are now better understood because of cultural analysis (Schein, 1985). In the past McGregor's (1960) analysis was about as far as anyone went in examining the topics of organizational perspective and atmosphere. For McGregor, all organizations were defined by how they stressed two particular considerations: task and interpersonal support for staff. McGregor's work led over many years to discussions of organizations that emphasized one or the other, and to the evolution of a norm, especially for human service organizations, which is a high level of emphasis on both.

Clearly, especially heavy emphasis on interpersonal support could reflect an organization's preoccupation with its own internal life. Such a skewed perspective might meet the needs of the workers, but it would impede the organization in assessing outcomes and in scanning and adapting to changes in the external environment. Conversely, excessive focus on task and problem solution can strain staff morale and lead to alienation over the long haul.

More recently, Cooke and Rousseau (1989) have suggested that organizations, as structures embodying and reflecting cultural properties, can be categorized into one or more of twelve cultural types. These types, which have their roots in McGregor's work, can be summarized as follows:

1. *Humantic-helpful culture*—Stresses people and participation in the organization. People are expected to help each other, to grow, and to invest their time and energy in each other.

2. *Affiliative culture*—Stresses a web of positive relations among people. Positive behavior in this culture means friendliness, expression of feelings, and recognition of the group's needs.

3. *Approval culture*—Stresses avoidance of conflict or even strong dissonance. People actively seek acceptance from others and feel the need to be liked.

4. *Conventional culture*—Stresses tradition and strong commitment to long-standing patterns. The structure stresses conformity and adherence to rules.

5. *Dependent culture*—Stresses the centrality of a few leaders within a vertical hierarchy. Participation is not promoted, and superiors are consulted before decisions are made.

6. *Avoidance culture*—Stresses the need not to fail or make mistakes. When people make errors, they shift responsibility to others for fear of being punished.

7. *Oppositional culture*—Stresses the rejection of ideas and of innovation. People's status is often tied to their criticism of ideas and others.

8. *Power culture*—Stresses nonparticipation by most people. Certain positions are key, inasmuch as they control those below them while giving the few positions above major attention.

9. *Competitive culture*—Stresses people's relative performance. Rewards accrue to performance winners, and people see themselves as working against others.

10. *Competence culture*—Stresses a relentless need to do everything, everything well, and everything on time. People are expected to do extra work, show persistence, and adhere to the structure.

11. *Achievement culture*—Stresses doing things well and promotes people who define their own goals related to organizational goals. Energy is focused within the organization and its members.

12. *Self-actualization culture*—Stresses creativity, uniqueness, and doing routine activities in outstanding ways. People are expected to grow as individuals, enjoy their work, and initiate new activities or meet new challenges.

Many social workers would be willing to give up almost everything, including higher wages, to work in an organizational culture where self-actualization is the norm. Unfortunately, the culture of many agencies is somewhere between competitive and a combination of avoidance, oppositional, power, approval, and conventional.

It doesn't take much time or effort to identify the primary culture of an organization. Nevertheless, culture is not easily influenced. It is not particularly permeable to either internal or external influences. It possesses all the properties of a norm—that is, it has a codified set of expectations, and it uses sanctions to enforce the culture and to resist change. While it isn't exactly the same dynamic, organizations fear and resist the unknown just as individuals do. They often will fight to maintain the status quo.

CONCLUSION

In this chapter we presented some of the basics of organizational life. Organizations can constrain and provide opportunities for practitioners. Organizations as social structures have properties and processes that can be positive or negative for practitioners and clients. Similarly, they have distinct cultures. In sum, organizations require practitioners to apply distinctive concepts so as to better understand and design practice responses.

CHAPTER 4

Working with Communities

Community is one of those abstract concepts that many presume to understand but, in actuality, see only as a complex mixture of definitions and descriptions. In this chapter we specify the factors that are germane to communities and to the practitioner who must solve problems in and with communities.

COMMUNITY AND ITS CHARACTERISTICS

Many noted theorists and writers are identified with the profession's present understanding of this rather elusive concept. A review of current thinking traces the idea of community to the classic writings of Ferdinand Tönnies, Max Weber, Charles Loomis, and Roland Warren. In the past, community has most often been defined on the basis of 1) geography (a specific area where people cluster or shared personal space); 2) size; 3) psychological considerations (interests, characteristics, social interaction); 4) sociological phenomena (shared interests, behavioral patterns, social interaction); 5) political power and governmental units; 6) ethnicity; 7) trade or commerce; and 8) religious affiliation.

After reviewing the numerous definitions available to the profession, we chose Warren's (1978) conceptualization of community as a social entity: "that combination of social units and systems that perform[s] the major social function[s] having [local] relevance."

Warren's definition is quite inclusive. Among other considerations, it addresses the "systems" issues on which we have built our understanding of macropractice. It also explores the issues of interaction and, while not stated explicitly, implies interdependence of actors. Finally, the definition speaks to locality in a way that addresses such issues as neighborhoods, space, ethnicity, race, and religiosity.

Against the backdrop of Warren's view of community it is useful to identify some of the major sociological and psychological concepts and theories relevant to this concept. Hardcastle, Wenocur, and Powers (1997) have identified several models and frameworks, discussed below.

Social Learning

Behavioral approaches to practice gave rise to the social learning theory. While it is more often identified with individual and group therapy, it provides a backdrop for understanding community-based practice. Social learning theory posits that behavior is learned through interactions with others. Those interactions can be with other individuals or with the environment. The contingencies of social learning are that

> to understand social action, social learning looks to cues that occur prior in time, mental processes (cognitions) that mediate them, and rewarding or punishing consequences that follow. There is also feedback from consequences to cueing and thinking for future behavior. (Hardcastle, Wenocur, & Powers, 1997)

Two other concepts important to an understanding of social learning are *perceived individual self-efficacy* and *collective efficacy*. Hardcastle et al. describe *perceived individual self-efficacy* as what individuals experience as they are able to determine and successfully carry out a goal-oriented course of action. When individuals fail to reach their goals and give up, it is called *low efficacy expectation*. For example, a practitioner who perceives pronounced community obstacles to a homeless shelter—strong work ethics or a very strong emphasis on self-reliance—might feel pessimistic about attaining community acceptance. Given this perceived social context, the practitioner might lower expectations of establishing a needed shelter. This response carried to its logical conclusion becomes what is called *learned helplessness* on the part of the practitioner. Those of us who have worked with community projects know the sense of futility that accompanies this behavior. It's tough, even for good and well-intended professionals, to move off "dead center" when this occurs. We find that we are not open to change because of our feelings of helplessness. We treat situations as though we have no power over them. In essence, we *react* rather than *act* in complex and often value-laden situations. In the example just raised, the practitioner might abandon all ideas of providing shelter and move toward furnishing bus tickets to the homeless in an attempt to move them to larger or different communities that do provide shelter care.

Collective efficacy is the shared perception that members of a group hold regarding their ability to achieve their objectives. The idea of *collective efficacy* applies to individuals who have come together in an integrated whole that is now more than the sum of its distinct parts (the individual group members; recall Lewin's ideas introduced in chapter 2). The group has its own energy and consequently establishes a shared perception of its efficacy and power as an integrated whole. Learning is a powerful dynamic in all social work practice. Practitioners spend much of their time attempting to understand and influence group member learning and its ultimate implications for group objectives. Sometimes the practitioner teaches new ideas and skills, coaches groups, and supports them; at other times the practitioner tries to undo self-defeating patterns of learning. Returning to the example of the shelter above, think of the dynamics that might operate within a committee formed to address the issue of the homeless.

Reality Construction

The theory of reality construction postulates that the social construction of reality is accomplished through social processes. In essence, objective facts only exist as individuals perceive and attach subjective meaning to the events with which they interact. Social construction cannot occur in abstraction or isolation. It can only occur as individuals are involved in concrete life experiences and interactions.

People live in a symbolic universe. Symbols are the means through which individual reality is developed. In particular, language (verbal, nonverbal, paraverbal) is critical to reality construction. "Language . . . helps to translate individual subjective experiences into objective reality and collective experiences into objective reality and collective experiences into cultural knowledge" (Berger & Luckmann, 1963). Thus our social order and interpretations of reality are created as people interact (talk, share experiences, validate each other) around shared expectations and goals. When people come together as a group, the group sometimes becomes *reified* (Hardcastle, Wenocur, & Powers, 1997). It develops its own culture, ideologies, and personality to the point that it takes on a life of its own. This life transcends its human origins and makeup. For example, the comment "You can't beat city hall" implies that "city hall" is something apart from the politicians and workers who constitute it. "City hall" has become inaccessible to particular people's efforts. One can appreciate how difficult it is to relate to any organization that has become reified. Who do you approach for change? What are the pressure points for change? The organization is devoid of feelings and emotion. It is less than human. In chapter 2 we suggested that you can't interact with and apply the same expectation of moral conduct to organizations, institutions, and communities that you can to individuals. The notion of reification sheds light on why it is difficult to tackle macrolevel systems.

Finally, reality constructionists believe that we internalize our reality through a process of socialization. Socially constructed realities are either stabilized or altered by the new information and alternative definitions constantly being received (Hardcastle, Wenocur, & Power, 1997). New information and alternative definitions of a given situation often create cognitive dissonance between the "established reality" and changing conditions, challenging established ideologies and beliefs. As a result reality construction allows the possibility of change. Reality, while not fluid or easily modified, is nonetheless dynamic and available to be changed.

It is important for social workers to enable clients to gain a greater degree of power over their lives. Reality construction can help practitioners to understand the positive uses of the group process and reification. For example, many people in "bad neighborhoods" have joined together to establish neighborhood watches and neighborhood patrols in an attempt to regain control of their lives. These are not vigilante groups, rather they are concerned citizens determined to take their neighborhoods back from drug traffickers, pimps, and prostitutes. Such acts of empowerment do work. These neighborhoods take on a new identity that makes it difficult for individual troublemakers to intimidate community members. The troublemakers must now contend with the will and power of the integrated whole. Moreover, the neighborhood's relations with other institutions also change. For example, it has been reported that police departments modify their views of such neighborhoods and actually become advocates for the citizens and their efforts at self-empowerment. The new reality is that the neighborhood can make a difference, replacing the old reality of individual helpless victims at the mercy of malefactors.

Social Exchange Theory and Power

Social exchange theory is less formal and easier to understand than reality construction, and it ties very nicely to much of the material already presented. This theory, which has its roots in behaviorism and economics, views the world through a framework in which large social units (groups, committees, boards) try to maximize benefits or rewards and avoid, or at least minimize, costs or punishments. Exchange theory suggests that social units who transact business review all possible exchanges and then select those that assure the greatest ratio of benefits to costs. The skills emphasized by this theory are bargaining, negotiating, advocating, networking, and marketing. Central concepts include an understanding of costs and benefits, which are linked to the ability to influence the holders of key resources. Any discussion of influence automatically introduces the concept of power. This fundamental dynamic will be revisited many times as we develop the knowledge, values, and skills of macropractice.

Social units that come together for purposes of exchange are interdependent and interactive. Interestingly enough, however, they are seldom if ever equal in power. Therein lies the problem. Those units with power invariably control the resources that other units need. Units that depend on other units must develop what are called "power-balancing strategies."

The five strategies identified with social exchange and power are 1) competition, 2) reevaluation, 3) reciprocity, 4) coalition, and 5) coercion (Hardcastle, Wenocur, & Powers, 1997). These strategies suggest some fascinating dynamics that can be quite disconcerting to practitioners. Coercion and competition both imply fairly high levels of conflict, which often makes practitioners extremely uncomfortable. Parties can end up in win-lose or, worse, lose-lose situations. Reevaluation, reciprocity, and coalition make more sense to most practitioners. However, workers may resist trying to develop such consensus among diverse groups of people because too much expenditure (waste) of time appears necessary.

Many social and behavioral scientists have studied the dynamic of power and the role it plays in effecting change.* Rollo May defines power as "the ability to act, to create change, and to influence others." He identifies five forms of power: exploitive—such as slavery; 2) manipulative—power over another person; 3) competitive—power against another; 4) nutrient—power for another, such as caring for one's children or loved ones; and 5) integrative—power with another (Bilken, 1983). May is evidently talking about individual influence rather than large unit or political power; however, his theory can apply to macropractice. Concepts such as exploitation, manipulation, and competition certainly have macrolevel implications, but May's list of five forms of power must be modified in order to be useful in understanding the behavior of larger groups. For example, Bilken criticizes May for not including consensus as a form of power, clearly suggesting that when a group of people agree on a course of action, they can have great power.

French and Raven (1968) wrote a classical article on the basis of social power. While their approach to and target of power is quite different from that previously discussed, their perspective is nonetheless quite helpful to our understanding of how power becomes the compelling form of influence. They identified five possible bases of individual power, which correspond closely to the five strategies identified in social exchange theory:

1. *Reward power*—The individual's power comes from the ability to administer positive consequences while removing negative consequences.

2. *Coercive power*—Similar to reward power, but there is an expectation that lack of conformity will bring punishment.

3. *Legitimate power*—A cultural belief system confers on the individual the "right" to have influence over others (conversely, others have a "duty" to follow that individual).

4. *Referent power*—The individual's power is conferred by others who respect and want to be liked by the individual; reward or coercion is not involved.

5. *Expert power*—The individual's power is predicated on knowledge, skill, and trustworthiness.

In 1970 Raven and Kruglanski (1975) added a sixth base of power:

6. *Informational power*—The individual's power is predicated on having the information needed to accomplish a given goal. The taxonomy of power

---

*Professionals use the terms "power" and "influence" interchangeably, as we will. Fellin (1987), however, takes issue with this use of language by defining power as "the potential ability of an actor(s) to select, change, [or] attain the goals of a social system, with an emphasis on "potential." In contrast, influence is the exercise of power that brings about change in a social system."

outlined by French, Raven, and Kruglanske applies to both the behavior of an individual acting as group leader and that of a group within a larger organization. For example, consider the value of understanding these concepts to a practitioner trying to facilitate interaction between a small neighborhood group and the local branch of Wal-Mart.

To end this section on power, it is useful to give Hunter's (1953) definition of power: "Power is a word that will be used to describe the acts of individuals going about the business of moving other individuals to act in relation to themselves or in relation to organic or inorganic things."

Hunter (1953) offered the following postulates:

1. Power involves relationships between individuals and groups, both controlled and controlling.
   Corollary. Because power involves such relations it can be described structurally.
2. Power is structured socially, in the United States, into a dual relationship between government and the private sector.
   Corollary. Both types of authorities may have functional, social and institutional power units subsidiary to them.
3. Power is a relatively constant factor in social relations with policies as variables.
   Corollary 1. Wealth, social status, and prestige are factors in the "power constant."
   Corollary 2. Variation in strength between power units, or a shift in policy within one of these units, affects the whole power structure.
4. Power of the individual must be structured into associational, clique, or institutional patterns to be effective.
   Corollary 1. The community provides a microcosm of organized power relations in which individuals exercise the maximum effective influence.
   Corollary 2. Representative democracy offers the greatest possibility of assuring the individual a voice in policy determination and extension.

The concept of power is often linked with such constructs as coercion, reward, legitimization, structure, and constancy. Recalling the discussion of Olson's view of social change in chapter 2, it is apparent that two key concepts keep resurfacing: coercion and incentive. Large structures may only change because of force or self-interest, but the group trying to bring about change had better have legitimacy and expertise or no change is likely to occur. Power is not something easily shifted or changed. Those in power are not willing to give up the benefits, clout, and resources associated with their power. This is what makes significant change difficult to achieve.

Conflict Theory

Conflict theory has its roots in the theories of Karl Marx and Ralf Dahrendorf. Its tenets are that

> (1) social systems systematically generate conflict, and therefore conflict is a pervasive feature of society; (2) conflict is generated by the opposed interests that are inevitably part of the social structure of society; (3) opposed interests derive from an unequal distribution of scarce resources and power among dominant and subordinate groups, and hence every society rests on the constraint of some of its members by others; (4) different interests tend to polarize into two conflict groups; (5) conflict is dialectical, that is, the resolution of one conflict creates a new set of opposed interests, which, under certain conditions, spawn further conflict; and (6) as a result of the ongoing conflict, social change is a pervasive feature of society. (Hardcastle, Wenocur, & Powers, 1997)

Marx saw conflict as arising from competition for resources. Clearly, he thought that when we talk about scarce resources, or when we talk about "the haves," and the "have nots," we are talking about power. In neo-Marxist theory power is tied not just to economic endowments but also to advantages associated with race, bureaucratic position, gender, sexual orientation, and so on.

Coser (1967) made an important contribution when he distinguished between "realistic conflict" and "unrealistic conflict." Realistic conflict is primarily conflict associated with a rational goal and concerns the means of achieving the goal. Unrealistic conflict, on the other hand, is conflict that is an end in itself. It springs from the irrational, emotional processes of the parties involved. These two dynamics can become important considerations in macropractice. When practitioners deal with irrational parties, those who simply want to disrupt or resist movement, little good can be achieved until the practitioners can find some common ground on which to build.

Conflict theory helps to explain, for example, why change efforts initiated by one agency may be opposed by other agencies in the community. Often those practitioners attempting to exercise influence are more committed to retaining their resources and improving their power base than they are to cooperating with or encouraging what they perceive to be competition. Basic to organizational, institutional, or corporate survival is the unit's ability to secure and maintain scarce resources. Only so much money will be allocated to social causes. Funds given to one program must come out of the pocket of another. Why should powerful agencies cooperate with someone else's project even if it fills an important unmet community need? Questions such as this suggest that at minimum, practitioners must frame change efforts as positive for the "losing" parties—as leading, for example, to better image or reinforced sanctions from the community.

COMMUNITY MODEL

This chapter began with Warren's definition of a community as a social entity. While Warren has not developed a systems model per se, he has constructed a model of how systems perform major social functions. He postulates that social functions are locally determined, and this leads to his emphasis on community functions rather than community institutions. Warren (1978) suggests that a community is characterized by the organization of the following five functions:

1. *Production-distribution-consumption*—Process of producing, distributing, and consuming goods and services. Goods and services are part of daily living, and it is desirable that they be accessible in the immediate locality.

2. *Socialization*—Process whereby prevailing knowledge, social values, and behavior patterns are transmitted to individuals. Through this process individuals learn to take on the way of living that is consistent with the community and not another societal unit.

3. *Social control*—Process of community influence that affects the behavior of its members and moves them to conformity with its norms. Several units will perform this function within the community.

4. *Social participation*—Process providing for participation within the community. Voluntary organizations, particularly religious organizations (churches and synagogues), are the most important units for channeling social participation. This does not negate the influence of other social units, such as businesses, government offices, and voluntary, public health, and welfare agencies.

5. *Mutual support*—Process providing support through family, neighbors, friends, and religious groups during sickness and economic distress and through the exchange of labor.

Communities in many areas of our country that have heretofore been identified as "rural" find themselves facing an interesting dilemma. It is called "urban sprawl." Large housing subdivisions and malls are crowding out open lands previously used for farming, for pasturing animals, and as wetlands for migratory birds. It is always disconcerting when neighborhoods suddenly find themselves surrounded by additional homes and poorly planned subdivisions. Unless the citizens of these unincorporated areas join together, there will be no greenbelts or open spaces and recreational complexes in developers' plans. Not surprisingly, parents find themselves wondering where their children can play little league baseball, soccer, softball, and so forth. New subdivisions can grow so quickly that even the location of schools becomes a point of contention. We see how Warren would regard this kind of unplanned growth: the profit motives of the land developers must be balanced by the public good and the needs of new homebuyers for readily available shopping areas, schools, recreational facilities, and churches—in short, for the functions needed to promote and sustain community life.

Warren's model adheres closely to the criteria previously developed regarding the multiple dynamics that facilitate social change. He uses much of the language of systems theory: concepts such as interdependence (production-distribution-consumption), interaction of actors (input and output of information is inferred), reference groups, transmission of norms, influence, conformity, power, and influence.

COMMUNITIES AS SOCIAL SYSTEMS

When considering social systems we must address structural interaction between two or more units (groups or persons). Parsons (1951) offers the following definition of those interactive dynamics:

> a plurality of individual actors interacting with each other in a situation which has at least a physical or environmental aspect, actors who are motivated in terms of a tendency to the "optimization of gratification" and whose relation to their situations, including each other, is defined and mediated in terms of a system of culturally structured and shared symbols.

Parsons's general definition provides a skeleton on which to develop a theory of systems. However, many other specific elements and dynamics must be included before the theory can be helpful in actually understanding a community. Loomis contributes a number of traditional constructs that are critical to a more dynamic view of social systems, especially as they may be reflected in communities:

> (1) *belief* (knowledge)—any proposition about any aspect of the universe that is accepted as true; (2) *sentiment*—sentiments are primarily expressive and represent "what we feel" about the world no matter why we feel it; (3) *end, goal, or objective*—the change or in some cases the retention of the status quo that members of a social system expect to accomplish through appropriate interaction; (4) *norm*—"more inclusive than written rules, regulations, and laws; they refer to all criteria for judging the character of conduct of both individual and group actions in any social system"; (5) *status role*—"that which is expected from an actor in a given situation"; (6) *power*—"the capacity to control others"; (7) *rank*—"equivalent to 'standing' and always [has] reference to a specific actor, system or sub-system"; (8) *sanction*—rewards and penalties meted out by the members of a social system as a device for inducing conformity to its norms and ends"; (9) *facility*—a means used to attain ends within the system. (Warren, 1978; quotes from Loomis)

Warren refers to Loomis's nine concepts as *structural elements*. He concludes, however, that to fully understand systems, one must also understand the processes through which organizations are given structure. Warren (1978) identified six processes that help to make social action and social interaction more predictable:

1. *Communication*—Process by which information, decisions, and directives are transmitted among actors and ways in which knowledge, opinions, and attitudes are formed or modified by interaction

2. *Boundary maintenance*—Process whereby the identity of the social system is preserved and the characteristic interaction pattern is maintained

3. *Systemic linkage*—Process whereby one or more of the elements of at least two social systems is articulated in such a manner that the two systems in some ways and on some occasions may be viewed as a single unit

4. *Socialization*—Process through which social and cultural hertitage is transmitted

5. *Social control*—Process by which deviancy is either eliminated or somehow made compatible with the functioning of the social group

6. *Institutionalization*—Process through which organizations are given structure and social action and interaction are made predictable

Reviewing and integrating the concepts above will help readers to better understand the utility of social systems. Readers will recognize certain properties that underpin the way they organize their thinking and the way they view the world. Parsons, Loomis, Warren, and others direct the thoughts and actions of practitioners through such concepts as boundary maintenance (open and closed), social interaction, systemic linkages, energy (tension and power), norms, sanctions (positive and negative), social class, social control, and institutionalization. These concepts and constructs are an integral part of the vocabulary of macrolevel practitioners, a part of everyday conversation and communication in macropractice.

GEMEINSCHAFT AND GESELLSCHAFT

Any discussion of community must at least briefly visit two concepts that have directed much thinking about community. Those concepts are *gemeinschaft* and *gesellschaft*, introduced in the 1870s by Ferdinand Tönnies, a German sociologist. In an attempt to discuss the community as a living organism, Tönnies drew a distinction between gemeinschaft, a warm, intimate, natural, emotive coming together for the common good, and gesellschaft, a rational, formal, cognitive association. For an intuitive understanding of these ideas, think about the stereotypical differences between rural, agrarian communities and large cities. Loomis, Beegle, Warner, and others have developed scales using the elements associated with Tönnies's original formulation (Warren, 1978). Figure 1 synthesizes the ideas of these authors in order to contrast these two important concepts.

While Tönnies's conceptualization of community has served social work practice well for several decades, it no longer fully explains life in the inner city, particularly in large urban communities. Daily life in communities where

Figure 1   Gemeinschaft versus Gesellschaft

Gemeinschaft	*versus*	*Gesellschaft*
Rural		*Urban*
Familial		*Contractual*
Nonrational—Sacred, traditional, affective	**Action**	*Rational*—Cognitive
Functional diffuseness— Activities are whatever needs to be done (What is the mother's job?)	**Range of Activities**	*Fuctional specificity*— Roles and activities are narrowly defined and are subject to specialization and specification
Community of fate— Complete responsibility (Your pain is my pain.)	**Range of Responsibility**	*Limited responsiblity*— (I'll do what I can, but I can't really be responsible. That's really too bad; I hope the fire deaprtment takes care of it.)
Required integration of roles in and out of the system — (What you do in private will affect your job.)	**Range of Roles**	*Roles outside specific system are irrelevant*— (What you do off the job is your business.)

Also We Have	
Primary, face-to-face relations	*Secondary, impersonal relations*
Personalized authority	*Impersonal authority*
Solitary	*Antagonistic*
Highly integrated roles	*Differing and even conflicting roles*
Interaction confined to the system	*Interaction distributed to many systems*
Determined by tradition	*Rationally determined by contracts*

people of color are the primary residents does not fit neatly into gemeinschaft-gesellschaft formulation. While these communities have more gemeinschaft than gesellschaft they are nonetheless different enough to merit their own classification. The new classification is known as *neo-gemeinschaft*.

A basic assumption of this classification is a powerless, minority community existing within a larger, antagonistic, and alienating environment. Unfortunately, many practitioners approach these communities with negative ("focused"), pessimistic attitudes. Empowerment and positive change can only occur, however, when practitioners approach these communities with attitudes that are positive and optimistic.

Rivera and Erlich (1981) view neo-gemeinschaft communities as primarily determined by racism and economic exploitation. They also suggest that these communities are closed systems, which has definite implications for individuals entering or exiting from them. It is easy to understand how such communities might be closed to individuals not indigenous to them. However, many social workers who have lived in neo-gemeinschaft communities are frustrated to learn that once they leave their neighborhoods and receive educations, their circles of influence decrease and can become inconsequential. In fact, it is not uncommon for members of the community to be unreceptive and even hostile to the "return of one of their own." They often view the personal accomplishments of the returning practitioners as a "sellout" to the hostile, larger system.

Rivera and Erlich postulate that daily life in neo-gemeinschaft communities is shaped entirely by the cultural, social, political, and economic interrelations within the community. Characteristics of such communities are

1. *Culture*—Homogenous; English may not be spoken; strong racial and cultural traditions; isolated from homeland; autonomous pockets within larger communities (often urban)

2. *Social structure*—Horizontal as opposed to vertical; shared experience of racism and oppression; strong extended family networks

3. *Power structure*—Mainly internally pluralistic; normally decision making by consensus; no trust of outside power blocks and their institutions

4. *Leadership*—Charismatic leaders ("personalismo"); strong feelings of alienation and anomie; sphere of influence limited to that community

5. *Economics*—Marginal level of existence; strongly interdependent; barter for survival; welfare is constant reminder of their situation; major players in labor market segmentation

6. *Physical appearance*—Strong ethnic flavor in signs, newspapers, and magazines; food from homeland; rundown tenements and substandard housing; mom-and-pop stores

7. *Social networks*—Strong and quite formal; networks integral to culture and horizontal support webs (Rivera & Erlich, 1981)

Practitioners working with these communities are "on the spot" until they prove themselves trustworthy. In order to be successful, workers must have knowledge and some experience with the community's culture, and it is critical that they be bilingual if they are from a different ethnic or cultural background. They must be able to relate to the culture and have respect for the networks intrinsic to the community. This presupposes that workers understand the coalitions in place, the power blocks inside and outside the community, the horizontal and consensual decision-making processes in place, and the role of age and wisdom as legitimate bases of leadership. Each neo-gemeinschaft community possesses a unique set of rules and governing principles, and it is the professional responsibility of the practitioner to understand them. Even more important, practitioners must feel comfortable and committed in working with these communities and their people. Caring, respect, and empathy cannot be faked when working with neo-gemeinschaft communities.

The following checklist may help practitioners to think through some of the central elements, dynamics, and the special considerations of communities:

1. Think of community, first, as basically a legal definition of locality and its associated populations.
2. Note carefully how social processes and patterns transcend those boundaries.
3. Understand how the community is an "arena" in which organizations perform much of the activity.
4. Understand how organizational interrelations cut across community boundaries. This is different from how rural residents interact with the community core. This concerns communities as "crossroads" for state, regional, national, and international organizational networks. Interrelations concerns also "vertical dimensions."
5. Understand that there is a certain kind of identification of persons with locality (partly a process of self-identification).
6. Think of all of the above as you consider the "entitivity" of the community. It can act as a unitary whole and as an arena for other things—people can get together as a whole city [entity] and vote down a school bond issue.
7. Recognize that within communities and between communities there is an ecology of spatial function as well as an ecology of other socioeconomic functions—zoning, banking, associations of governments, and so forth.
8. Map the functions and demographic characteristics of the community. This often accounts for why the rich live together, the poor live together, and the ethnics choose to be together.

ECONOMIC AND POLITICAL POWER

We have raised the idea of power on a number of occasions. We will now develop the concept more carefully in order to bring it into a practice context. Power has several different components that practitioners must understand, and the various dynamics associated with power must be central to their thought and behavior processes (Meenaghan, Washington, & Ryan, 1982).

There are essentially three types of power: positive, negative, and potential. *Positive power* comes from an individual, group, or institution as that social unit attempts to accomplish something it values. *Negative power* comes from a social unit as it attempts to block another unit's efforts to accomplish a goal. Negative power exists only when positive power is counteracted (by a negative power).

Positive power cannot always be harnessed. Social units (some of which are very complex) don't always support even good causes just because it is moral or ethical for them to do so. They must have a "good" reason to support any given initiative—where "good" means "in the unit's interests." The best situation the practitioner might be able to negotiate with a given power unit is that it won't oppose a specific change initiative and use its negative power against the effort. In short, it will stay neutral and not interfere.

The third type of power, *potential power*, is the one macrolevel practitioners find themselves most often attempting to access. Practitioners are forever scanning and screening the community for potential power sources. The same individuals or institutions are not necessarily appropriate as power sources for every project. Individuals and institutions with power also have their own agendas and special interests and will not "buy in" to just any project. It is critical that practitioners understand the resources that constitute power. The most relevant are "financial assets (land, dollar, businesses, investments, and the like); status (organization and institution position, family name and position afforded by people of area); and, increasingly, information and linkage to other powerful people" (Meenaghan, Washington, & Ryan, 1982).

These resources are both earned and inherited, and they are not static. Family name or family wealth has a much different dynamic than status, for example. Status is much more fluid than inherited wealth. One reason groups may reach out to a practitioner as a community organizer is the status the practitioner has earned within the community as a professional. It is conceivable that the practitioner has achieved high status through hard work, professional integrity, knowledge of the power structure within the community, knowledge and skills, personality, and overall energy and expertise brought to community projects. In essence, the practitioner has become a source of power within the community.

Over the years, a three-part classification has been developed to describe the configuration of powerful people in a community:

1. *Elitist structure*—Disproportionate power resides in the hands of a few people.
2. *Pluralist structure*—Several different people have power, and they will coalesce; however, their coalitions are issue specific.
3. *Amorphous structure*—There appears to be no persistent pattern in the way power is shared in the community.

If not careful, community practitioners find themselves forever trying to understand who the elites are within a community. While this is critical for some communities, for others considerable effort must be exerted in understanding one of the other two power structures (Meenaghan, Washington, & Ryan, 1982).

Dahl (1962) offers interesting insights into the elite group, so often the focus of attention. He refers to them as "economic notables," and he describes them as a unified group of citizens who determine "policy" through meetings and negotiations held in the privacy of their clubs, homes, offices, and other closed places. His notion is of a "covert," or clandestine, exercise of influence that comes from wealth, high social standing, and economic dominance. These elites are the "real" leaders of the community because those holding official positions and public office represent the interests, values, and perspectives of these power sources.

Dahl also identifies an "overt" power elite in a community, made up of religious, educational, and economic leaders who are open about their dominance and power. Overt power brokers are in fact no easier to work with than those who are not as open about their dominance. They may be more accessible, but the end result is much the same. The practical strategy is to access the power elite through its repesentatives, and through those linked to them. For example, a practitioner who has no direct access to a powerful U.S. senator may have access to a key political leader at the state or county level. The practitioner can frame a request within a context of political exchange tied to the ongoing interests of both political figures.

Over time, the term "power structure" has crept into the professional jargon (Hunter, 1953). It has become a generic expression for many of the complexities we are discussing in relation to power, influence, and social control. Issues of order, form, and convention (structure) are suggested by the term. In fact, practitioners often refer to the "formal" and "informal" aspects of the power structure. Simply put, *formal power* is based on custom and convention and is often linked to position. Formal, positional power is hierarchical in form and dynamics. Practitioners must often negotiate a vertical chain of command to reach the individuals or groups they desire to see. Such attempts to access formal power often involve a tedious, structured, restrictive process. Once a practitioner arrives at the desk of the formal decision makers, however, the power there is real.

Practitioners working with organizations that have middle-level managers must be especially careful. Many middle-level administrators are "climbers" in their organizations and, as a result, can be very insecure in their positions. Practitioners should not normally try to "end run" around one of these people unless they are prepared to pay the price. Middle managers may not have the power to assure the success of a practitioner's project, but be assured they often have enough power to scuttle the project. While practitioners may need to reach decision makers above middle managers, these managers should not be blindsided or made to look bad. Practitioners should involve them enough in the change process to gain their support and should pass them some of the accolades from whatever success is achieved.

Informal power, on the other hand, is based, not on positions, but on access to formal power brokers and decision makers. It remains somewhat camouflaged and is not always easily identified because people with informal power may or may not be in the official "chain of command" of the power source the practitioner is trying to access.

Informal power might best be understood with a short vignette. A mental health advocacy group needed to reach the governor to express its concern about the mentally ill homeless in one of the state's large cities. All attempts to communicate with the governor through formal channels were thwarted by her staff and advisors, who didn't want her sidetracked on a matter with so little potential political gain. The group located a personal confidante of the governor's and through him arranged an early morning breakfast meeting just before the opening of the annual legislative session. During the meeting it became apparent that the governor's staff was managing the information being provided to her and that, as a result, she had no idea how serious the mentally ill homeless problem really was in that state. The governor attached a million-dollar clause to her "state of state" message in an attempt to address the problem. The governor's staff and advisors were not pleased when they learned their system had been breached; however, they did nothing to incur the further anger of the governor.

Let's step back now and take a second look at the mixed dynamics of formal and informal power. It has already been stated that each community has elite and other leaders who hold the key positions (business, educational, corporate, religious, and political) and thus represent the formal power structure. However, the power you need to tap might not always rest in the most obvious positional location or with the most obvious individuals or groups. The mayor, city commissioner, or county commissioner of the community may have a position of significance; however, cumulative experience may tell the practitioner that this official has very little real or dynamic power. The worker will therefore need to identify those individuals, groups, or organizations in the community who really make things happen. This means discerning the community's informal power structure by finding out who, directly and indirectly, can influence other community actors.

Meenaghan, Washington, and Ryan (1982) postulate three ways to explore and identify community power. In the *reputational method* the macropractitioner convenes carefully selected "panel of judges," who are then invited to identify the power brokers who will be most helpful in assuring the success of a given project. The key to success in this method lies in the selection of the panel. The members must be a cross section of the community. Some should be long-time community members, some should hold positions of note. Once the panel has compiled a list of power brokers, it could be asked to rank order the individuals identified according to their ability to influence outcomes.

The *issues analysis method* is a variation of the reputational method but is more complicated. Four or five current issues or concerns in the community are first identified. The list of concerns can be generated in a number of ways; the process need not be formal. A list of key power brokers is then developed for each concern. These lists are then cross-referenced to see which people show up across more than one concern. If the practitioner sees a different group of people for each concern, a pluralistic power structure is likely present in the community. If the same people show up on the different lists, there is a good possibility that the practitioner is dealing with an elitist structure. Whatever structure emerges must be factored into subsequent deliberations and practice responses.

The *positional method* equates power with positions or titles. This approach is somewhat crude because power doesn't always reside in identified positions, but it has the potential to get a project started. Although it shouldn't be used alone, it is a good approach when combined with one of the two methods discussed above.

We close this section of the chapter by talking about the practice considerations implied by the three power structures described above. First, elitist communities have the following identifying characteristics:

1. Power is held disproportionately by a few individuals.
2. Leaders are often geographically and socially removed room the bulk of the community.
3. Elites do not generally come from the professions; they are more often associated with intergenerational wealth and position.
4. Elites avoid publicity.
5. Elites are active on issues that affect their interests and resources.
6. Elites lack direct connection to organizations.
7. Elites come from a narrow range of occupational positions.
8. Elites tend to have strong points of view concerning human services.
9. Certain elite families evolve into roles of being guides to the community.
10. Voluntary and private organizations tend to be valued by the elites.

11. The social process used by elites tends to be predictable and informal.

12. The social process tends to represent special interest groups.

13. The social process is inclined to certain political positions. (Meenaghan, Washington, & Ryan, 1982)

These thirteen identifying characteristics are the backdrop against which practitioners plan their activities within the elite community. This is not the easiest power structure to work with. Facilitating change with these power brokers necessitates a conscious review of the incentives that might be brought to bear as well as any coercive tactics that might become necessary. Reason suggests that one would not start with coercion. Note how the thirteen characteristics translate into practice considerations:

1. The community is stratified, exhibiting little linkage across layers. The layers basically involve a) elites, b) professionals and organizations (public and private), and last c) citizens at large.

2. Elites are isolated, not necessarily informed of needs, inclined to be cautious about any change, and structured into viewing the present state of affairs as basically adequate.

3. Professionals and formal organizations are inclined to be aware of their lack of power and their ultimate dependence on and conditioning by the elites. They likely push certain issues and see only certain goals as realistic or possible.

4. Citizens-at-large are uninvolved and isolated from the elites. Without power in any real sense, they at best are linked indirectly to the professionals and formal organizations in the community.

5. The basic problem the practitioner and his or her organization encounters is the structured inertia. The people or groups who need or want changes will typically not have power; those who do will often not see the need for change or perhaps will resist it. Similarly, lack of information about different people and groups, stemming from social separation and inadequate communication patterns, can suggest no action on behalf of people for acceptable reasons, via acceptable programs.

6. The practitioner then has to assume some responsibility for acting as a catalyst to activate the stratified system.

7. This means that the practitioner has to assess the issues that an organization wishes to pursue as being neutral, positive, or negative in the eyes of the elites. If an issue is neutral toward or even supportive of the interests of the elites (including the need to be paternal guide), then strategies of selecting information being presented to elites through intermediaries, education, and the like should be pursued. In short, compensatory communication strategies should be considered. (Meenaghan, Washington, & Ryan, 1982)

Clearly, change can occur in elite communities, but social workers must understand the delicate line they walk. However, while there is need for caution, pessimism can be fatal to change efforts. Excessive caution and screening out of desired goals are two reasons why elite communities are slow to change and why elites retain the power. In the words of General George Patton, "know your enemy;" however, don't be intimidated by them to the extent of paralysis. Respect their power and influence but refuse to be controlled by it.

Pluralist communities are not totally different from elitist communities. A main difference is the stress pluralists put on the public sector. They make room for the contributions of professionals and the public political process. The system is more open and public, and therefore, groups must recognize their potential power in the decision-making processes of the community. In pluralist communities, power brokers and decision makers are more often subject to community accountability and sanction. Pluralist communities have the following identifying characteristics and consequent practice considerations:

1. There are few key people in a given decision or issue area. The community does not look to the same key (elite) people as power brokers on *all* projects. Power is distributed broadly.

2. Powerful people tend to come from three institutional sectors: industry and business, government, and the professional world. Moreover, they tend to come in approximately equal ratios; that is, no one sector such as business or banking clearly and routinely dominates. The practitioner should get involved in board work and community activities immediately. It takes time to become established as a significant actor.

3. Power tends to be specialized and key people are often involved in decision-making arenas because of occupation, profession, and organizational affiliations. The result is not only that power is restricted in scope but that the goals and interests of such people tend to be focused and at least indirectly related to constituencies that sanction their use of power. For example, the school superintendent has power largely due to organizational position. This power has distinct parameters, and the superintendent's goals are not unrelated to the interest of key constituencies such as taxpayers, teachers, and so on. This same superintendent may have significant influence on country- or state-level educational boards and committees based on reputation, knowledge, and skills, but not necessarily within the communities of the school district, and not across issues other than education. Remember, the people of the specific school district are his or her boss.

4. The power of groups and group interests can be maximized by the use of collective pressure and coalitions. Such practice-related activities can help to integrate different groups and segments of the community. They can also help decision makers, especially public decision makers, to identify

significant groups and their interests and goals and then to make decisions that positively link them to key groups and their agenda. Such decisions then become investments in developing or maintaining key constituency support. (Meenaghan, Washington, & Ryan, 1982)

The approach often used with pluralist communities is that of informing and educating those with power in order to promote the ideas and activities the practitioner is undertaking. Powerful actors are approached by many
groups with good causes, and they must choose where they will invest their
time, money, and energy.*

At times, however, the practitioner must move beyond educational and
informational strategies. Often the practitioner will try to form coalitions with
other interest groups or power brokers in an attempt to bring increased pressure to bear on key decision makers and the decision-making process. It is necessary to understand that this strategy can be fraught with problems. Support
is not a one-way street and the practitioner can be sure that these interest
groups and power brokers will expect support in the future. Sometimes the
price of support from certain groups is simply too high for the practitioner to
bear. Indeed, coalition-building tactics are political, and relying on such influence can sometimes backfire. This is why practitioners need to anticipate the
outcome and costs of forming coalitions with groups that may later make
demands detrimental to the practitioners' organizations. Practitioners always
need to know the risks associated with certain strategies, and they have an ethical responsibility to inform key constituencies and supporters. While the belief
that all politics is dirty is incorrect, all concerned parties must weigh the costs,
risks, and potential benefits very carefully. This caution also applies to the way
practitioners use the press, courts, and other resources in an attempt to move
power brokers. Unsophisticated people are often quick to go to the media in an
attempt to get at individuals, groups, or organizations that are unsympathetic
to or blocking their "pet projects." They may think they have won the battle
after a particular press release, but they ultimately lose the war. Power brokers
and politicals have a way of "steadying the ship after the first volley."

One very important point remains to be made with pluralistic communities. It has to do with the nature of the issue on which the practitioner is
focusing. If the project is the subject of high, positive consensus among the
power brokers, education-oriented strategies are the preferred practice
options. If, however, the project requires a redistribution of status, rewards,
and role prerogatives, then a politically oriented strategy is better. The dynamics operating here were alluded to earlier. Simply put, powerful people do not

---

*The same holds for a practitioner as a community professional. Once established and identi-
fied as a person with possible influence, the practitioner must choose very carefully what boards
and committees to join. If the practitioner really does have power, and access to power, many
groups will want the practitioner's services, reputation, and influence.

willingly give up resources (wealth, power, position, etc.), even for good causes. By using the political process the practitioner engages the community where it is understood that there must be some give and take and that there are times when it may cost something to meet the community good.

Finally, there are times when an important power group sneaks up on the practitioner. For example, most communities have a strong "gray panther" group of the elderly. They may not be visible as long as no one in the community tries to "cut their grass"; but let someone propose an initiative that will affect them adversely and personally and it becomes clear why they are called gray panthers. Communities usually try, insofar as possible, to find win-win resolutions to power struggles. People hate win-lose results, especially when they perceive themselves as the losers. So, for example, it may be crucial to remove as much personal cost to the elderly (often on fixed incomes) as possible when attempting to float a substantial school bond. The elderly can be expected to go only so far in their altruism and desire to provide for the youth of tomorrow. At the critical point of self-protection or self-interest they will organize against bond measures. Invariably, the suggestion of new taxes brings a reaction from the gray panthers.

Amorphous communities are very difficult to study and understand. Some community systems are problematic simply because they are amorphous. These communities lack structure and are generally in flux, between elitist and pluralist structures. Because of this, it is difficult to tap community power, and consensus is not always an option. In such communities, diversity can very quickly polarize citizens and the decision-making process because legitimized power exists to help stabilize the process. Meenaghan, Washington, and Ryan (1982) suggest that "since the amorphous community is in a kind of vacuum, then the best... practice approach to the situation is (a) to recognize the vacuum, and (b) if necessary, to assume an assertive role to attempt to maximize organization or group interests."

Conflicting agendas are at play in these difficult communities. Long-time residents invariably try to protect their "turf" and the traditions of the past. They are very sensitive to losing something they value, something to which they feel entitled.

Such communities can be quite vulnerable to the few who get together and plan for the future. At times, through the complacency of the majority, some less than popular decisions are imposed on the community simply because "the few" get their act together first, get involved, and move out with a plan. This is an example of how the "silent majority" gets caught napping, thinking that a few instigators will not have the power needed to pull off their plan.

Our discussion of power has focused on the importance of understanding how critical this particular dynamic is to ultimate success in practice. Power is an ever-changing construct and can be very fragile. It requires support in the from of cooperation and obedience. It is not very durable, monolithic, or protected form change and influence. It is fascinating to watch as former power brokers try to reenter a previous arena of influence. Many times their support base has eroded and they no longer have access to formal decision makers. For example, former deans and directors of schools of social work can be heard discussing the dynamics of what happens to them after they step down from their administrative positions and roles. Though they retained some status and recognition, they invariably lose power. This loss is evidenced by the fact that they no longer have direct access to the college president, the governor, or the mayor or that they are no longer invited to sit on important policy-making boards. The power they enjoyed was assigned to them by community power groups and brokers. When a former dean or director can no longer bring title, position, and resources to the decision-making arena, that person's particular expertise is no longer needed. This is especially true in pluralistic communities.

Because power has its source in people and can and does change, it belongs to no one exclusively. Groups come together in mutual action and can influence social process by either supporting or withholding cooperation, support, and obedience. These same groups can join together and create new entities (agencies, services, etc.). Hannah Arendt (1959) made a significant observation about power: "Power is always as we would say, a power potential and not an unchangeable, measurable, and reliable entity like force or strength." Power doesn't lie around dormant, patiently waiting to be called on. Some power brokers assume their power is ever present and unchanging, only to find in a specific skirmish that they have no clout with the particular group they want to influence. In fact, power brokers sometimes wander onto foreign turf and find the constituency openly hostile. A common example is when elites attempt to "step up" (through their assumed power) and overly direct people.

Power does not rest directly on resources such as money or property; rather, it rests on the significance given to such things. One reason the rich have power is that some broad range of the public perceives a need for some of their wealth and is willing to act in a way that obtains it. The rich often use the nonrich, thus establishing power; and the nonrich often use the rich, thus assigning them even more power. Interestingly enough, the poor, as consumers, can exercise power by refusing to buy select products from the rich. The same point can be made about authority that has been made concerning money and power. Power and authority both depend on the support of people in order to be valid and viable. Chester Bernard (1965) contends that contrary to conventional wisdom, "the decision as to whether an order has authority or not lies with the person to whom it is addressed, and does not reside in persons of authority or those who issue orders." Bernard's observation implies the importance of empowerment and self-empowerment. Specific individuals only have power over others if the "others" elect to assign them that power (Bilken, 1983).

KEY ELEMENTS OF COMMUNITY CULTURE AND HISTORY: WHAT CHANGE IS POSSIBLE?

Perhaps it sounds obvious to say that a successful practitioner must have comprehensive knowledge and understanding of the community; however, this is not as simple as it seems. Real subtleties at play in a community can keep a worker off balance for inordinate amounts of time and until the delicate intricacies are better understood.

Because many elements come together in the fabric of any given community, different social work writers have conceptualized the types of communities in different ways. For example, Brueggemann (1996) identifies three kinds of communities: 1) modern, 2) ontological, and 3) traditional. Rubin and Rubin (1986) also identify three kinds of communities, but they have conceptualized them as 1) traditional, 2) solidarity, and 3) neighborhood. Interestingly enough, both sources distinguish the traditional community, and while they use different terminology, they specify essentially the same elements and characteristics in ontological and solidarity communities.

Looking at each kind of community separately we can begin to ferret out their most distinguishing elements. *Traditional communities* are almost a thing of the past. These communities have their roots in rural areas, and while they still exist today they are more or less enclaves of the past. Many third world countries, Native American tribes (Navajos are a classic example), the Amish, and the kibbutzim of Israel provide examples of traditional communities. These communities are characterized by commonality, belief set, ritual commitment, and social bonding that exceeds what is commonly found in most modern communities. There is a sense of identity and interdependent responsibility that simply is not supported in larger, more complex communities. For example, in Navajo communities there is an unspoken claim that goes with being a tribal member. Members are expected to look after one another and share their means as needed. The elderly are revered and respected well beyond courtesy, and even deference. When children are orphaned or when there are problems within families, grandmothers and aunts immediately step forward. Another way of expressing the dynamics of this type of community is the old African proverb "It takes a whole village to raise a child" (Brueggemann, 1996). While residents of traditional communities interact with society in general, they do so on their own terms. They do all in their power to remain free of the control of larger societal institutions. These communities vary in their ability to maintain their uniqueness and autonomy, but they remain deeply committed to the values, attitudes, ideologies, philosophies, beliefs (often religious or spiritual), and sense of purpose that unites them.

Solidarity and ontological communities have close ties to traditional communities. They tend to exist within the infrastructure of larger, more complex modern communities. Again, these are communities of people with a common heritage. That heritage can be religion, language, race, ethnicity, culture, or other social property. These communities are identified by their emotional, spiritual, altruistic, compassionate, and caring commitment to community members. Invariably, a sense of self-protection exists within these communities. They, like traditional communities, try to protect their own against outside interference. Brueggemann suggests that these communities prize justice and stand strongly for their convictions.

The people of these communities can be very assertive and, indeed, almost radical in their determination to maintain their unique identity and sense of well-being. They are often identified by religious affiliation, political leanings, and philosophy of the good life. These communities are not all "flaming liberals" or " radical right-wing conservatives," but they nonetheless are very strong in their beliefs and commitments and as such can have strong influence on local politics. Many are starting to flex their muscles more than in the past. It is partly their voice that pushed for welfare reform, the restructuring of the IRS, and the proposed emptying of Lake Powell and Lake Meade. They tend to align themselves with political parties that are sympathetic to their causes and concerns. For example, some ethnic groups in large cities, while quite conservative about family and cultural values, may vote for Democratic candidates because of the party's standing concern about jobs and the greed of the corporate world. These citizens often look to the government to protect them and to assure entitlement programs. On the other hand, citizens in some rural states tend to vote Republican because of their disdain for organized labor and governmental intervention. They insist that there is plenty of work for those willing to work, and they support this contention by citing the work ethic of the "green card" migrant workers who labor in their fields and vineyards. While solidarity and ontological communities and their members can be powerful voices and have great potential for organizing around common concerns, practitioners have to be careful about the complexities of their values, their reasons for wanting change, and their resistance to change.

Modern communities are very complex in their makeup and dynamics. No two cities are exactly alike, even when they have similar characteristics. Within large modern communities are found neighborhood districts, ethnic neighborhoods, planned community living, low-income districts, homeless districts, school districts, towns, villages, business districts, office buildings (sometimes a corporate headquarters), shopping malls, industrial districts, railroad districts, and factories. Many large communities (cities) find themselves with shrinking or depleted economic and tax bases as "the money" leaves the center and moves into the suburbs. Central city communities and neighborhoods often struggle with high rates of absentee ownership. Many modern communities have attempted urban renewal and developed "planned living communities" in an effort to lure the wealthy back into the central city. They have tried to revitalize their shopping districts and to make it safe for individuals to come into the community for shopping, recreation, and entertainment. The sense of community produced is often limited and rather transitional, in terms of time and movement of people.

Many large, complex communities suffer from a sense of alienation and anomie (normlessness). Individuals do not generally know one another, and there is no real sense of community or community spirit. Because society is so mobile, people tend to resist putting down roots in such communities because they perceive themselves as strangers. On occasion they might even view themselves as interlopers. Individuals pursue much of their activity—work, recreation, social life, religious observance, shopping—outside the community. Brueggemann (1996) maintains that "alienation breeds loneliness, fear and lack of identity with others." Modern communities can also breed separation and even oppression. Lines become clearly drawn between the haves and have nots. For example, people in the affluent planned communities often live behind locked gates and heavy security systems to protect themselves from the rest of the citizens. Once such lines are drawn, stereotyping and other processes can oppress those who are not members of power groups.

The *neighborhood communities* of America are also in transition. In years gone by, neighborhoods were the place where we grew up, the place where we went to school, and the source of our loyalties and personal ties. Over time these neighborhoods often lose their loyalties and personality because the young grow up and move away. Nonetheless, neighborhoods can still be a significant source of power. While interpersonal relations tied to shared residential space may not be as prevalent, neighborhoods can develop an interdependency that focuses on mutual problems, concerns, and common interests. When this happens, people come together on an issue-by-issue basis (Rubin & Rubin, 1986).

Warren (1978) contends that as we have moved away from a folk-urban distinction and sacred-secular polarity to more interdependent communities (no longer self-contained units that can provide all goods necessary to the community) a number of changes have occurred. He identifies these changes as consisting of a new division of labor, a differentiation of interests and association, an increasingly systemic relation to the larger society, increased bureaucratization and impersonalization, a transfer of functions to profit enterprises and government, urbanization and suburbanization, and, finally, changing values. Most of Warren's points have been addressed in our discussions of the various theories and views of community. However, three need to be developed.

Many people discuss *bureaucracies* as if they are the great dragons of our day. There are obviously problems in trying to relate to bureaucracies, but practitioners need to appreciate the real strengths linked to the discipline and rigor bureaucracies introduce into problem-solving activity. Weber (1946) has described bureaucracy as having a rational character: rules, means, ends, and matter-of-factness dominate its bearing. He has suggested that practitioners must discipline themselves to be rational in their approach to large units (institutions and organizations) rather than to just make emotional appeals. Emotional appeals are rarely more than "water off a duck's back" to matter-of-fact bureaucratic power brokers. While the arguments a practitioner makes may have some emotional force, they had better be pragmatic and substantive in content. Remember, bureaucracies primarily weigh costs and benefits, not feeling.

A second of Warren's points that hasn't yet been fully developed concerns the role and nature of *private nonprofit and public social service agencies*. It is essential for practitioners to understand attitudes toward the use of social welfare and human services in the communities where they work. Some communities have little or no confidence in the "good will" of people and, as a result, have little faith in voluntary associations. They put their trust and well-being in the hands of the public sector. On the other hand, some communities will not use public agencies (participation paradox). Rather, they feel comfortable only using private nonprofit agencies and voluntary associations. Individuals in these communities may only avail themselves of services provided by the United Way, religious organizations, or community centers that are basically organized and staffed by volunteers. This preference is often accompanied by great hostility about the level and quality of services provided by public agencies. In fact, a movement currently well under way encourages state-level social service agencies to privatize most of their services.

A third area identified by Warren is *societal and community values*. Values are not static; rather they are continually in flux. Even at those times when values are perceived to be fixed and unchangeable—or perhaps especially at those times—some community decision will be reached that shocks almost everyone involved. John Williams (1951) developed an excellent four-point outline for appraising the importance of different and possibly changing values:

1. *Extensiveness* of the value in the total activity of the system. What proportion of a population and of its activities manifest the value?

2. *Duration* of the value. Has it been persistently important over a period of time?

3. *Intensity* with which the value is sought or maintained as shown by effort, crucial choices, verbal affirmation, and reactions to threats to the value— for example, promptness, certainty, and severity of sanctions.

4. *Prestige* of value carriers—that is, of persons, objects, or organizations considered to be bearers of the value. Culture heroes, for example, are significant indexes of values of high generality and esteem.

Note the components of this classification. Extensiveness, duration, intensity, and prestige are key concepts relative to values. In America, the values that have stood the test of time in most communities are individualism (almost to a fault at times), democracy, success, education, and happiness. Values related to such areas as sexual orientation, sexual activity, abortion, and planned parenthood are somewhat more fluid. Practitioners should not assume they know where the community stands on a particular value or set of values. However, they do need a sense of the value issues the community will support and those the community will resist no matter what. For example, some communities may be very supportive of AIDS research and hospice care yet resist any effort to redefine the family through legislative action that would legalize gay marriage.

CONCLUSION

In this chapter we explored the complexities of community. From an introduction of a community's salient characteristics we proceed to some of the major social science perspectives on communities. The systems frameworks of Warren and others received extensive focus. The dynamics and reality of power in communities was stressed especially in terms of resources, processes, and consequences for practitioners and change efforts.

CHAPTER 5

Entering and Assessing Communities

In evaluating the many faces of communities, practitioners will find themselves drawn back to the generalist practice framework developed in chapter 2. The first construct we introduced there was the systems framework. We also introduced problem solving as an integrative practice model. Essential elements in using problem solving as a practice model are critical thinking, rationality, disciplined approach (orderliness), data gathering, and analysis.

As practitioners view communities as social systems, various elements come into play, including beliefs, values, norms, roles, status and rank (social stratification), power, and sanctions. In addition, practitioners evaluate the processes of communication, systemic linkages, boundary maintenance, the nature of socialization, the nature of social control (attempts to create or sustain equilibrium), and other similar dynamics.

As we move to dealing with communities, it is useful to cite Warren's (1978) systems questions:

> (1) What units make up the "community system?"; (2) To what extent can the community as a social system be distinguished from its surrounding environment?; (3) What is the nature of the structured interaction of units in the community as a social system?; (4) What are the tasks that the community performs as a social system?; (5) By what means is the structured relationship among the interacting units of a community maintained?; (6) Can an external and an internal pattern of activities be differentiated in the community?; and (7) What is the relation of community social-system units to other social systems?

Warren doesn't presume to know what constitutes a community in the context of a given practice. Rather, he invites the practitioner to define the community as it impinges on particular interests and concerns. Are such communities as the Polish and Italian sections of New York City neighborhoods, localities, or ethnic groups? The people of these ethnic communities can transact almost all their daily activities in their native languages.

Further, Warren doesn't suppose that any community is exactly like other communities of equal size. And communities with similar sociodemographics may differ greatly because of religious or political values. Rather, he suggests that every community is a unique entity. For Warren, it is necessary to understand the boundaries (geographic, psychological, etc.), that exist within and between the community units, that the practitioner has identified. The nature of the boundaries and their permeability (openness vs. closedness) greatly affects a practitioner's ability to facilitate interaction with the units under consideration. Boundaries are intended to assure the integrity of the community. They exist so that the values, norms, beliefs, and way of life can be kept undiluted. Consider the ethnic neighborhoods of America. They are dedicated to the preservation of culture, religion, language, and the sovereignty of the family. For example, consider how the boundaries in an Amish community would differ from those in a rural railroad town. Railroad towns usually have great racial and ethnic diversity, so they must learn to deal with diversity. An Amish community, on the other hand, would be slow to welcome people or ideas that would dilute their values or way of life.

In addition to boundaries between various units, practitioners must consider the structured relation among interacting units. For example, the Amish community and the railroad town would also differ in areas of exchange and governance. Much less money may be exchanged in the Amish community. Bartering and the exchange of goods and services may be more typical. Economic activity may be more cooperative and less competitive. The railroad community, by contrast might be more modern. It is also likely that the Amish would govern themselves through a theological lens and not through a democratic political model.

Finally, Warren urges practitioners to pay attention to vertical and horizontal patterns within the community. These concepts have to do with the relation of community social system units to other social units. For example, nationally operated chain stores are not free-standing entities in given communities. They relate vertically to a district office or corporate headquarters. The relation between the two is hierarchical, and as a result, the extracommunity corporate office has substantial power and authority over the local store. This can become a problem in a community when the corporate office is insensitive to local norms, beliefs, or values. A typical problem in many religiously conservative communities in America is the issue of "Sunday closing." Despite the preference of some communities that local stores and businesses be closed on the Sabbath, many national chain stores tend to disregard the wishes of these communities and even the advice of their own local managers. The result is an atmosphere of uneasiness, disequilibrium, and tension. These communities often feel paralyzed, unable to act against these large corporations. They behave as if they are powerless. The other side of this coin can be found in Israel, where Orthodox Jews (a minority of the country's population) are able to influence the closing of businesses. These two examples illustrate the important distinction between power and size.

Horizontal patterns are reflected in the relations among social units that are on essentially the same hierarchical level (Warren, 1978). These patterns are as important as vertical patterns. The absence of a hierarchical relation between units does not guarantee cooperation. For example, a practitioner might expect that two agencies funded by the United Way (say, a family support and treatment center and a women and children in crisis center) would support attempts to set up an intermediate residential living center for abused women and children. However, they may have something to lose by supporting new initiatives. United Way funds may be limited, and the development of a new agency or program would no doubt affect the funding of these two agencies.

ASSESSING COMMUNITY TYPE

Each community has a different face and can be defined in a different way. Meenaghan, Washington, and Ryan (1982) provide six systematic techniques for specifying the type of community: the rural method (spatial/institutional), the corporate, and statistical area methods (spatial), the social area analysis method, the interactional approach, and the systems approach.

Rural Method

Even practitioners who will never work in rural or semirural areas should be conversant with the unique dynamics that define communities in these settings. The *rural method (spatial/institutional)* is associated primarily with low-density rural areas. Land grant universities (University of West Virginia, Michigan State, Kansas State, Colorado State, Oregon State, etc.) and associated extension agencies have for years systematically studied these areas. They are the experts at understanding what constitutes a "community" in most rural areas. They also are knowledgeable about the belief sets, values, and power brokers typical of rural communities.

Interestingly enough, public health, mental health, and welfare agencies also have had to become familiar with rural and semirural culture. The reason is the Community Mental Health Center Act of 1963 (P.L. 88-164), inspired by President John F. Kennedy and signed by President Lyndon B. Johnson. The language of the original bill was in great part intended to address rural America. Its use of such terms as "catchment area" meant that rural towns, small cities, and even counties were expected to come together in cooperative and interdependent associations in order to qualify for federal money. In this way rural populations gain access to costly mental health, public health, and other services that rural towns and counties of free-standing farms and ranches are in absolutely no position to offer alone.

Small rural towns are often as competitive with nearby communities and have boundaries as closed as some neighborhoods in large, diverse cities. They will identify and protect themselves in the same way as some groups in the inner cities. Typically, these small rural towns are not inclined to let some official from a different county have any say over them and may even resist officials from their own county. These towns often worry about bigger entities taking advantage of them and yet won't coalesce or cooperate with other communities. Autonomy and identity are critical elements of their culture, and practitioners must be sensitive to their presence and role.

It is easy to assume that power brokers and influential individuals in very similar communities will be essentially the same kinds of people, but this is not always the case. In one rural town decision-making power might be entrusted to a school superintendent, a church leader, or a doctor. In another town, fifty miles away, the decision maker could be the mayor or the police chief. In some communities, leadership is held by groups such as fraternities, clubs, and orders. The leadership of the Grange, Masonic Lodge, Moose Lodge, or Rebecca's might have the power to direct the entire community.

Practitioners involved with rural or semirural communities where a number of towns are spread across several counties can use the following procedure:

1. Secure a good map of the area, with towns and roads identified.

2. Identify the names and locations of all towns, boroughs, and cities. Focus on the larger legal bodies that the towns must relate to, such as the county seat.

3. Develop a number of plastic overlays that show important focal points: businesses, schools, hospitals, agencies, and so forth. Use a color code for this essential data: different colors for large corporate offices, public buildings, private nonprofit agencies, hospitals and so forth.

4. Visit the various towns and identify specific organizations associated with major institutions: banks, health centers, commercial enterprises, educational units, religious influences, social service agencies, governmental entities, and so forth.

5. Create index cards or computer records with names of agencies and businesses and the key players, by name and position in each unit.

6. Try to talk with people from each of the units identified. Select senior or upper level personnel, and be sure to choose people with longevity in the community.

With this homework accomplished, the next steps of the problem-solving framework can be tackled. The first is to provide a "clear statement of the problem." This may sound easy, but it often isn't. The problems practitioners address sometimes defy being stated in a simple, straightforward manner. Community problems reflect very complex and varied issues and interests. What may start as a fairly clear and concise need may suddenly balloon into a project of such magnitude that the likelihood of studying it or responding to it successfully is very low. For example, a practitioner addressing the needs of abused women and children doesn't have a simple task of goal selection. What is the practitioner and agency going to focus on? If the practitioner works in a small community with limited resources, is the agency going to try to provide a "full purpose" response that includes a safe house for both women and children? Will the agency provide clinical services, housing services, job services, and legal services? If not all of these can be done, what will be taken on first? Will the response be to provide shelter for the victims and to work out clinical services elsewhere, or will the response forgo the safe house and push for better legal support and professional counseling? The "wish list" is always bigger than the practitioner's ability to produce. Practitioners must know clearly where they are, where their projects are going, and what the goals of their projects are.

Corporate and Statistical Area Methods

The *corporate and statistical area methods (spatial),* are not especially good ways of understanding communities. We introduce them, however, because they are so widely used. In and of themselves the methods do not give practitioners the information they need to properly understand community type, but they do help practitioners to get started. These methods provide a nice backdrop for beginning practice responses.

The *corporate method* views the community as a physical entity created by law or administrative rule. For example, a city may become incorporated under the auspices of the county or the state. Once incorporated the city is then responsible for such services as police and fire protection, water provision, library services, road repair, and so forth. These kinds of services are fairly straightforward and easy to understand. However, other administrative entities cut across city or county boundaries and are not as easy to grasp. For example, there are administrative entities created by law, bonding requirements, or contractual agreements that are designed to serve citizens within designated geographic areas whose boundaries don't necessarily coincide with those of other entities. Many communities come together to provide such services as unified school districts (county high schools), water treatment districts, health and mental health delivery systems, and recreational facilities (swimming pools). The catchment areas formed to qualify for federal comprehensive mental health funds are another example. These forged relations can be quite tenuous, because fierce rivalries often exist within these entities. For example, counties containing only small communities (towns of under 1,000 residents) will not see eye to eye with counties containing cities of 300,000 on many issues, and cooperative efforts between them could become very difficult and painful. Meenaghan, Washington, and Ryan (1982) warn that special arrangements cutting across city and county boundaries tend to hide the subtleties and variations of people living within these areas. These purposefully created units are "communities" of administrative convenience and not entities that meet the criteria of more homogeneous, intimate communities previously presented.

A human service organization will have difficulties if it treats a particular corporate community as if all its citizens are the same when the corporate community is in fact highly heterogeneous. This error can be particularly problematic when small or diverse units are annexed to a large metropolitan corporate entity.

A final limitation of looking at corporate entities as communities is the misleading impression of stability this gives. In fact, communities and their residents change over time, and social service agencies must keep abreast. For example, an agency may have been established to support and strengthen young families. Over time, however, the community may become a haven for retired and semiretired people. The agency now finds itself confronting the needs of an aging population that it may or may not be prepared to serve.

The *statistical area method* is a product of the times. The federal government, confronted with the need to manage large grants, has relied on a system of identifying communities, in terms of catchment areas, that now seems rather arbitrary. Government agencies often provide grants intended to serve people from such areas that fulfill specific population requirements. Those requirements include minimums and maximums for the catchment area and, on occasion, will dictate mileage restrictions as well. For example, participants may be required to live within fifty miles of where the services are provided in order to qualify for service. Obviously, the citizens within a given catchment area may have very little in common. One segment of the "community" may be completely agrarian while another may be made up of highly educated light industry employees. While it is fair to be critical of this method, it is a political reality that many social service agencies are required to serve communities identified in this way. Practitioners and their agencies must recognize the limitations of the method, as well as the issues it raises, and then design sensitive and compensatory practice responses.

Social Area Analysis Method

A fourth method for understanding community type is the *social area analysis method,* which is derived from a sociological community assessment method known as Shevky-Bell social area analysis. "While the rural method stresses the community as a place within which functions occur, and the corporate/statistical methods stress community as place within defined boundaries, this method stresses the population characteristics of people who inhabit the land" (Meenaghan, Washington, & Ryan, 1982).

Social area analysis stresses the social and economic characteristics of the community being studied. Human service organizations do not have to gather these data themselves because the Census Bureau collects a substantial amount of such information every ten years. Shevky and Bell have developed an elaborate statistical procedure that reduces the voluminous data received in census reports to usable information on the families, economics, ethnicity, educational levels, and workforce of a community. Practitioners can approach the census data using their methodology:

1. Mark out the very broad boundaries of the area that your organization serves and that you wish to understand better. For the purposes of our discussion, assume that your agency is in the community mental health arena and is considering opening two outpatient satellite offices in a catchment area that covers 800 to 1,000 square blocks within the city. Immediate issues and questions present themselves in terms of site selection, range of services, staffing, and so on.

2. Go to the census reports that include the tracts for the broad area in question, and consider looking at the tracts in terms of such social economic variables as rent, educational level, and occupation. The logic behind the use of these items is clear—generally, the more money you have, the more you will pay for housing; the higher your income, the longer you stay in school or the more likely you are to select certain occupations. For family variables, consider such items as rate of single family residences, fertility rate, and number of women not in the official labor force. (Obviously, data on fertility and women not in the labor force are riddled with issues of relevance and applicability due to changes in society.) Finally, for ethnic variables, consider such items as race, nativity, and number of ethnically linked surnames.

3. Operationalize definitions of family, economic, and ethnic properties. Consistently apply these definitions to all tracts. Typically, you would select a particular variable for each of the three factors. For example, consider all tracts by single-family residence rate, educational level, and race. Then convert the percentage values of each of the three variables to scores on a four- or two-point scale.

4. Since each tract's three scores speak to distinct characteristics, you cannot add them together after you have scored them. Instead, you should now look at the tracts—individually and collectively—in terms of the composite scores. This allows you to distinguish different types of social areas. To do this, take the pair of family and economic scores for each tract (using the suggested four-point scale); there are sixteen distinct possible pairs. When you also consider ethnicity, scored on a two-point or four-point scale, the number of possible triples of scores is either thirty-two or sixty-four. Thus the variables chosen and scoring system used allow thirty-two or sixty-four community types.

5. Examine all tracts' scores, and identify those tracts that are similar/dissimilar, especially among those that are contiguous. Where patterns of scores are the same for contiguous tracts, you can assume, using this

method, that the combined area constitutes a community. When noncontiguous tracts score the same it is assumed that these tracts are distinct but have some things in common because their population characteristics are alike. At this point, you can say how many types of communities exist within the catchment area.

6. After the tracts are scored, and types of communities identified, you can selectively use social science research to guide practice decisions. Social science has much to say about what problems are likely to affect different types of people at different stages and how different types of people use organizations—where "types" of people are conceptualized according to family, economic, and ethnic characteristics. For example, areas that have high family scores are probably more interested in school-related concerns, while areas that have low economic scores are not apt to respond well to formal organizations and long-term group projects. (Meenaghan, Washington, & Ryan, 1982)

Interactional Approach

Though many experts do not consider it systematic enough to call a method, the *interactional approach* to data gathering is very helpful in revealing important qualitative aspects of communities. Data do not have to be quantitative in order to be valid. Indeed, the interactional approach yields qualitative data that are extremely helpful in understanding the formal and informal processes of suburban areas and ethnic enclaves within larger settings. Equally important, the interactional approach helps differentiate between one area and another, between one population and another, and it can help practitioners to see how different groups and people sort themselves in terms of the roles they play.

In 1959 Greer and Kaufman offer a construct they call "limited liability" that sheds light on the interactional approach. Simply put, they believe that people, even when they live close together, share the same land, and move in the same neighborhoods, do not have to relate to one another, the area or local institutions in a uniform, determined way: people have a lot of latitude in how they conduct themselves. While practitioners may regard this as case scenarios, it poses some organizational dilemmas. How does a practitioner know what to do and who to contact to get a project off the ground? For example, what is the "division of labor" in a particular community? Greer and Kaufman identify three key roles played by the citizens of a community: actors, neighbors, and isolates.

Actors are the movers and shakers of the community. They are deeply involved in community activities and devote a lot of their time and energy to the welfare of the community. They often live and work in the community, and many own businesses there, which clearly means that they have an investment in its economic and social viability. They belong to the chamber of commerce and Rotary Club, serve on the school board, and are contributing members of the United Way organization. They interact significantly within the community, are deeply committed to the area, and may have much to lose if community life goes stale. These people are very important for practitioners to get to know. They can be identified through the methods we discussed in chapter 4 for assessing persons of power and influence.

The second role, *neighbors,* is one most of us know well. Neighbors interact socially with people around them, particularly with those with common interests. They may associate around school or church, youth sports, and other activities located in their immediate neighborhoods. They do not get involved in the community to the extent that actors do; however, they will get together in their limited relations. These people can be very helpful to practitioners in planning and organizing activities, but typically, practitioners must reach out to them. They aren't usually committed to larger community policy and often won't care about general issues initially. Neighbors need a good reason to get involved, but when they do, they can be quite powerful. These are the people in the local news who decide to "reclaim their neighborhoods" and rid themselves of drugs, prostitution, and violent crime. They can become very serious about neighborhood watches, patrolling the streets, carrying cell phones, and generally serving notice that they are involved. Neighbors can make a difference; yet once things have quieted down, they will often slip back into their less visible role.

Isolates "are in an area, but not of it." For whatever reason these people feel no sense of community. They are often viewed by community leaders and actors as transient and uncommitted. They rarely view themselves as a permanent part of any community and so see no need to get involved. In some instances, isolates are the ones who need the social services that agencies provide. While isolates may be slow if not impossible to get involved, their needs and considerations must be entertained in order to have an accurate representation of the services your agency may need to offer.

Fellin (1987) offers an interesting discussion of six types of neighborhoods:

> *Integral neighborhoods*—Have cosmopolitan ties as well as a local center where individuals are in close contact. Individuals from these neighborhoods share many concerns and participate in community activities. These neighborhoods have a high capacity to identify problems and take action because of their extensive internal organization and numerous links to the outside community.
>
> *Parochial neighborhoods*—Have strong ethnic identities and homogeneous character. They are self-contained and independent of the larger community. They screen out whatever does not conform to their own norms. Because of strong group identity (race, class, age, physical isolation, etc.) these neighborhoods have social integration,

a strong commitment to the locality, and the capacity to get things done even without outside help. Their functions may be limited by lack of linkage to the larger community.

Stepping-stone neighborhoods—Have high levels of activity but play a game of "musical chairs." Residents participate in neighborhood activities not because they identify with their neighborhoods but because they want to get ahead in their careers. They demonstrate a lot of self-serving behavior but are very transitory occupationally, socially, and residentially; hence these individuals do not identify strongly with the "neighborhood" even though they may be positive about where they live. Residents of these neighborhoods are on the move and do not expect to be in the area for long. These neighborhoods are not conducive to long-term relationships.

Transitory neighborhoods—Have pockets of high rates of change. Population change is occurring. People break into groups such as "old-timers" and "new-comers." Little or no collective action or neighborhood organization takes place. There are no mechanisms for dealing with turnover. Residents use the broader community as their reference point, have little capacity to deal with change, and become almost immobilized at prospects of social disorganization.

Anomic neighborhoods—Have no cohesion. They are in fact "nonneighborhoods." They demonstrate significant social distance and have no protective barriers against outside influences. They are responsive to some outside change but lack the ability to mobilize and organize for common action. Such neighborhoods either in low-income public housing or in luxury condominiums.

Diffuse neighborhoods—Have many things in common and are often quite homogeneous (new subdivisions or inner-city housing projects). However, they have no active internal life and are not tied to larger communities. They have little involvement with people in direct physical proximity. They possess a high degree of collective capacity to act but don't do so. Residents do not feel they need the neighborhood for help or social interaction.

Systems Approach

The *systems approach* to gathering data about the community and its functions is similar to the interactional approach. We have already discussed this approach, but we need to return to the Loomis, Sanders, and Warren material one more time. The systems approach focuses on the functional processes of the community and the structural entities associated with these processes. It is a way to examine qualitatively the division of labor in the community. Recall Warren's assertion that in order to understand the communities with which they work, practitioners must understand the five processes that shape those communities: production-distribution-consumption, socialization, social control, mutual support, and participation (see chap. 4 for details).

Within the systems approach, these major functions of the community must be viewed in light of four major systems differentiation constructs: goal attainment, adaptation, integration, and tension management. Obviously, each community differs in the ways these functions are manifested and the ways local structures interact. That's one reason practice in larger systems is so exciting and challenging. Warren ties all of this dynamic material together by outlining how communities can be understood in terms of how their basic functions relate to the four sources of differentiation:

1. *Autonomy*—The degree to which the local area is able to perform all of the basic functions; the degree to which translocal bodies and processes are necessary. For example, how possible is it for a rural railroad community to meet its needs in a county inhabited by second- and third-generation farmers?

2. *Coincidence of service areas*—The degree to which the physical spheres of different service providers coincide. For example, how much do banking areas overlap with school district areas, mental health catchment areas with local council of government areas?

3. *Psychological indentification*—The degree to which there exists a positive, collective tie of people to land, and people to people within shared physical boundaries. What did the Native Americans of the Phoenix, Arizona, area feel as lands adjoining their reserve became prime vacation and retirement locations for the wealthy and elderly?

4. *Cohesion*—The degree to which inhabitants are behaviorally and socially linked to each other via informal or formal relations. What problems might be associated with cohesion as a sizable number of people move into a community that was predominately made up of people of one religious persuasion—especially if the long-term residents conduct all business, civic, and school affairs within the context of the predominant religion? (There was a time when an Irish-Catholic could not hold political office in Boston.) All of these dynamics affect cohesion. (Meenaghan, Washington, & Ryan, 1982)

The biopsychosocial dynamics of Warren's approach are a fascinating mix of micro- and macrotheory. They suggest that practitioners must be cognizant of individual and small group considerations as well as large system dynamics. For example, practitioners must be aware of the interpersonal (micro) characteristics of the people they work with, paying attention to mutual support, participation, psychological identification, and cohesion. In addition, practitioners must attend to the macrolevel dynamics of production-distribution-consumption, socialization, social control, autonomy, and coincidence of service areas. Practitioners must next add the four dynamics that speak to how systems function: goal attainment, adaptation, integration, and tension management. This conception of an interplay of functions and differentiation gives practitioners a viable tool for understanding the personality, complexity, and will of communities.

CONDUCTING COMMUNITY STUDIES

We now turn our attention to four common ways in which community studies are conducted: field study, community power structure study, community analysis, and dual problems and services studies.

Field Study

Field study has been around for a long time. It is sometimes regarded with disdain because it is less scientific than other methodologies. Moreover, properly conducted field studies can be very time consuming. Simply put, in a field study the researcher is a learner, obtaining information by interacting with community residents, who are the experts with knowledge about the community. Field study researchers often immerse themselves in the population under study for months in an attempt to understand the community through the unique eyes of community members. This is qualitative research, and this particular process is called "naturalistic inquiry." It occurs face to face and is a very hands-on and humanistic approach to data gathering.

Field study is a particularly good approach to diverse populations, neighborhoods, and communities. The sociocultural mosaic that can be constructed from one of these studies is invaluable. The key to success with the approach lies in the practitioner's ability to establish relations with community members, to relate in a trusting, caring, concerned manner that acknowledges each person's dignity. This demands from the practitioner an openness, unpretentiousness, and ability to validate others, even people who might not seem of particular note or who are not deemed important by community leaders.

Hardcastle, Wenocur, and Powers (1997) point out the importance of working with "key respondents" or "key informants" in conducting research. They are careful to emphasize that these individuals are key because they are well positioned in the community to act as interpreters for the practitioner who is gathering information; these individuals are *not* necessarily indigenous or elected leaders and are seldom if ever professionals. They are simply people who know and understand the community and will share their knowledge and expertise with the practitioner. They can be brought in at various points in the study and will help to keep the process and outcome "honest."

Daley and Wong suggest that practitioners engaged in a field study "are learners, not experts coming in; [they and their] informants will share, affecting each other and the process, so there is emphasis on interchange, 'mutual learning,' and 'respect'" (quoted in Hardcastle, Wenocur, & Powers, 1997). Information is gathered by listening, keeping journals and field notes, making tape recordings, observing, and conducting ethnographic interviews using structured and open questions. The material collected can become voluminous and difficult to interpret. This is one reason practitioners must confer with their key informants about tentative assumptions. In addition, many practitioners use "content analysis," a statistical procedure, in an attempt to detect patterns and commonalities among the community's concerns (Rubin & Babbie, 1997).

Community Power Structure Study

The spirit and many of the elements of *community power structure study* were presented in chapter 4. As Hunter, Dahl, and others have noted, the power structure methodology has introduced into the professional vocabulary such terms as "the powerful," "the elite," "influentials," "dominants," "power brokers," and "power actors."

In this approach the practitioner must understand the nature and structure of power in the community, especially in terms of key influentials and the roles they might play. Hardcastle, Wenocur, and Powers (1997) have developed a set of questions that can be used to understand the power makeup of a community:

1. Who runs this town?
2. Who are the most economically powerful persons?
3. Who controls the resources?
4. Who determines local taxes such as real estate taxes?
5. Who benefits?
6. What is known by everyone concerning the power brokers here? Are there others operating behind the scenes?
7. Does anyone with connections at the county or state level live in the subdivision, neighborhood, or town?
8. Who is influential due to the high regard people have for them or because of their clout with politicians?

These questions can be posed informally to colleagues and other people who have lived and worked in the community long enough to have an idea of how it works. The practitioner could also use one of the more formal methods discussed in this chapter. Answers to these questions help the practitioner to determine who to approach within the larger system.

Practitioners study the influentials of a community in one of three ways: in terms of their reputations, in terms of the positions they hold or in terms of their ability to influence decisions. Each influential can be assigned to one or more of three groups, depending on the answer to the following question:

"Is this person (1) perceived to be powerful, (2) occupying a position that confers authority and power, or (3) actually involved in specific decision making?" (Hardcastle, Wenocur, & Powers, 1997). All three power groups have strengths and weaknesses. Usually, no individual completely dominates the activity of a community; however, if the practitioner detects the "loading," or recurrence, of an individual in at least two of the three groups, the practitioner has identified a key person who should perhaps be approached, directly or indirectly.

To identify all influentials in the community the practitioner must include the names of agency directors, business owners, public officials, corporate leaders, church leaders, foundation leaders, school leaders, civic leaders, and board members of all leading community organizations. After this positional list is complied, the reputational or issues analysis method can be used to determine who the real power brokers are (see chap. 4). Remember this is done by convening a panel of respected, generally recognized community leaders and having them develop a ranked list of influentials. (Hardcastle, Wenocur, & Powers, 1997) suggests that the practitioner then interview the thirty or forty top ranked people and ask each person what ten individuals make the key decisions in the community and to rank order them in terms of their ability to influence and lead others. The practitioner can then consider the people identified in terms of their relevance to particular issues or problems, their access to particular influentials, and the manner in which they should be approached.

Let us illustrate how positional influentials can help practitioners to obtain the information needed to develop new projects. A study undertaken a few years ago in the United States and Israel selected like communities to see how health, mental health, and other social services were provided in what were called "dead zones," areas sufficiently high in crime and drug activity to make it dangerous to deliver services to the residents. Large maps of the cities identified in the study were presented to police chiefs, fire chiefs, and social service directors. Each of these key informants was asked to outline vulnerable areas by street, block, or neighborhood. After all interviews were completed the maps were compared. Interestingly enough, the individual maps varied very little; the critical areas were clearly identified. These positional leaders knew their communities extremely well and thus were an invaluable source of information for the researcher.

Community Analysis

Community analysis is a newer approach to the study of communities. Less defined than the two approaches already discussed, it is sometimes described as "getting the pulse of the community." While not as rigorous as field study and community power structure study, it provides enough information to permit the practitioner to move forward. Quite frankly, this approach is usually chosen because of time and resource constraints. Hardcastle, Wenocur, and Powers identify community analysis as a broad interpretative study based on factual documents as well as interviews with officials and natural leaders. Community analysis also uses observation and research methods. The approach includes a "once over lightly" examination of particular problems or issues and the groups involved and the development of an initial impression of what powerful groups and individuals influence the life of the community. The analytical work starts when the practitioner refines these initial impressions.

Unlike a field study where the practitioner starts with people at the neighborhood level, community analysis starts countywide or citywide and works down to smaller units. To use this approach the practitioner needs not only city maps, but all available printed material on the community and its neighborhoods. Such material includes names of banks, major businesses, and social service agencies; political and community histories; descriptions of notable community programs; community member impressions; and reports and studies from other organizations. The practitioner also needs any secondary data available: census material and other sociodemographic data (crime rates, income, etc.). Hardcastle, Wenocur, and Powers (1997) suggest that once a practitioner gets to the streets to interview the citizens there is no longer any need to be concerned with power actors. The practitioner should just talk with anyone and everyone—gas station attendants, schoolteachers, fast-food employees, small business owners and employees, anyone with something to say. Typical questions that might be asked are: What are the boundaries of this community? What do you call it? Do old-timers call it something else? Where do people stop to chat, hang out, or relax around here? Have you ever seen anything written about this area? Should I read it? What are the good and bad points about living here? What special problems or central issues does your community have? Who are the important civic leaders in the community and why? Who are the chronic gripers in the area? What are their complaints?

Obviously, this isn't a one-day activity. Even though this process uses a sample obtained by happenstance, practitioners must do their preliminary work. During one community analysis, the practitioner asked key community influentials where residents turned for mental health services. The answer was most interesting. This was a small rural community, and residents, especially the influentials, were hesitant to discuss "such personal matters." The leaders simply said they didn't have mental health problems in their town, even though they were aware that a prominent physician's wife had committed suicide only three years before. When the practitioner asked regular townspeople the same question, however, it quickly became apparent that people were driving fifty miles to a large city to receive services, so no one in the community would know of their illness. When the new mental health center opened, the need for services in the community easily matched the conservative national estimate that 10 percent of society struggles with mental health problems. The key leaders protected the reputation of the community by not knowing or revealing what was happening to their neighbors, while the nonelites and noninfluentials knew and were willing to talk about the problem.

Hardcastle, Wenocur, and Powers (1997) have developed a brief but effective format for gathering the data discussed above. As the data are collected and then analyzed, practitioners should cross-check their analyses with informants.

Sample topics to be explored:

a. demographic considerations;
b. corporate players;
c. jurisdictional boundaries;
d. demographics (race, ethnicity, income, etc.), statistics, subgroups;
e. story of community and neighborhoods, community strengths today;
f. political structure, governance;
g. economic structure, major or key employers;
h. social services structure (public agencies, non-profit agencies, extent of service availability);
i. mutual aid (churches, clubs, orders, fraternal organizations), community action organizations;
j. potential/actual civic and service problems; and
k. power relations (consortium or political dyads).

Sample approaches to be utilized in conducting a community analysis: (a) interviewing, "hearing" the community in new ways; (b) observing, analyzing (critical thinking skills); (c) collection illuminating anecdotes and stories; (d) following methods used by social scientists; (e) providing orientation materials (maps, photographs, visual material that tell a story); (f) being aware of personal bias (know self, own feelings, understand and acknowledge limits of analysis.) (Hardcastle, et al., 1997)

Dual Problems and Services Studies

Dual problems and services studies both pinpoint and evaluate the services needed to address them. They are generally used to assess special populations. For example, a practitioner may be focusing on the immunization of the children of migrant farmworkers. Consider how complicated it might be for the practitioner to obtain the information needed to act responsibly in this matter: Have there been systematic immunizations? Are there shot records? Where are the records? Can the families speak English? When you do problems and services studies you will usually be invited to do exploratory or evaluative work or some combination of the two.

These two kinds of studies—problems and services—differ from those presented earlier in that they do not look for the common denominators in a community. Rather, these studies focus on the distinctive features of people with a particular problem of a particular group that is oppressed or disadvantaged. Think of the concerns a practitioner would address, the questions the practitioner would ask, and the homework the practitioner would do before successfully helping those in a community suffering from AIDS. Imagine the pain and frustration that would come in trying to work with and on behalf of this client group. Practitioners must sometimes count on hostility and prejudice. Yet there are critical human needs that should be met with compassion and sensitivity (Hardcastle, Wenocur, and Powers, 1997).

MAKING NEEDS ASSESSMENTS

A human need is any condition that keeps an individual or family from realizing their full potential. These needs are usually identified and understood within a social, economic, or health-related context. Meenaghan, Washington, and Ryan (1982) identify four aspects of quantifying needs:

(1) The need represents an identified social, economic, or health related problem of individuals and/or families; (2) The problem affects categories of individuals (or families) with similar characteristics; (3) Persons affected may be located in a defined geographic area; (4) The identified problem may be directly addressed by some current or future service that may be provided by an organization or individual.

By far the most popular and exacting approach used in community evaluation is *needs assessment*. Typically, when conducting needs assessments practitioners gather quantifiable data that reflect the condition of a specific population within a specified area. To carry out this process practitioners must integrate much of what we have presented in this book. For example, return to the problem-solving approach and the absolute need to determine an objective:

1. Begin the project with a carefully conceptualized objective.
2. Define the study population and develop an appropriate methodology for conducting the study—that is, determine what data are to be collected and select the sampling procedures.
3. Choose an appropriate contact method for gathering the data—face-to-face interviews, telephone contact, or mailings.
4. Develop the instrument, usually a questionnaire. It is prudent to pretest the instrument to make sure it gathers the information needed. An untested instrument can generate costly errors and even cause the process to fail.
5. Organize and conduct the survey itself.
6. Process and study the data (both statistically and analytically).
7. Report the results. (Hardcastle, Wenocur, & Powers, 1997)

By thinking critically the practitioner is likely to reduce errors in the data-gathering process. The process is thus strengthened against challenges.

For a more detailed description of needs assessment, it is useful to consider the six steps identified by Franczyk. These steps build on and support the material presented above:

Step 1. *Selecting units and topics for analysis.* Initial action involves the identification of target groups (populations at risk) and/or the geographic area about which information is to be gathered. These target groups and geographic areas are known as the units of analysis. The kinds of information desired about each of these units are the topics of analysis.

Step 2. *Selection of one or more methods for gathering data.* A choice must be made between establishing an ongoing, agency based, informational system or implementing a short-term data collection project. The advantages of using existing data must be weighed against the costs of generating new data.

Step 3. *Gathering data/generating information.* Information about the needs of the specific units of analysis is generated from the aggregation and analysis of the individual bits of data collected.

Step 4. *Identifying unacceptable social or human conditions.* Having formulated a composite picture of the conditions experienced by the units of analysis, certain conditions are judged to be in violation of acceptable standards.

Step 5. *Comparing observed conditions to existing services.* Data collection on community needs is compared to information about the availability, adequacy, and effectiveness of existing services in meeting these identified needs

Step 6. *Recommending changes in existing services.* The product of a well done needs assessment should be a confirmation of existing services as adequate or recommendations for change to cope with the observed inadequacy. (Sheafor et al., 1997)

Note the critical concepts identified by Franczyk: (1) identification of population and problem and (2) relevance of differential risk among groups and areas. Practitioners are required to identify and select "populations at risk" and actual problems that the community feels need attention. This does not mean that practitioners won't at times need to *educate* a particular target group about the seriousness and dysfunctionality of a particular situation in its community. However, the target group must perceive a problem, must feel some discomfort (tension/energy), and, most of all, must want to address this issue.

Alternative Approaches to Needs Assessment

There are alternative approaches to needs assessment. Before we move deeper into the mechanics of needs assessment let's review the approaches identified and summarized by Kimmel:

1. Gathering Opinions and Judgment
   a. key informants
   b. community forums
   c. public hearings
   d. community and political leaders
   e. group processes—semi-structured activity

2. Collecting Service Statistics
   a. utilization of data and rates
   b. caseload and workload data
   c. grievance and complaint data
   d. waiting-list data
   e. service data in existing management information systems

3. Epidemiological Studies (systematic studies of the origins of problems)

4. Studies of the Incidence and Prevalence of Problems (e.g., disease, handicapping conditions or defects)

5. Social Indicators—Use of quantitative measures of the variables (e.g., unemployment, crime, schooling, income housing, etc.)

6. Survey
   a. formal general population sample survey (by telephone, mail, or in person)
   b. formal sub-population sample survey (e.g., locality, age, or service population)
   c. Selective special interviews with service clients, providers, practitioners, agency officials, etc.

7. Secondary Analysis of Existing Studies or Sets of Organized Data

8. Combinations of the Above (quoted in Kramer & Specht, 1983)

We now discuss some details that must be considered when specific approaches are used.

Developing the Questionnaire

The next step in the process of needs assessment is developing the questionnaire. Many problems and errors can occur in attempting to articulate what it is that needs to be known. Questionnaire construction is not easy, and practitioners may need to consult more experienced colleagues until they have enough experience to stay clear of the land mines that await. Following are some basic rules of thumb:

1. Know what you're after, and don't ask for information you don't need. Generally, questions must relate directly to your objective. This is not the time to elicit unrelated information. Keep the questionnaire short, to the point, and directed to action.

2. Respondents should have a reference point for receiving the question-naire. The questions should make sense to the participants and seem important to them. Questions should focus on a community problem with which the respondents are already acquainted and want to solve.

3. Know your audience and aim the questions at the education and background of those being surveyed. Do not talk down to people but do not rely on overly technical language or unfamiliar terms; avoid professional jargon.

4. Be very careful about the wording of questions, and do not ask two questions at once. Questions should be focused, specific, direct, clear, and easy to answer.

5. Don't ask leading questions. Leading questions skew answers in a particular direction and presuppose a right answer.

6. Avoid long items; avoid complex items that, even if not double barreled, may be confusing.

7. Avoid the use of negative terms such as "not" since people will often overlook the negative modifier.

8. Keep the answer categories as simple as possible. For example, give respondents a short list of clear choices to pick from. These are called "fixed format questions," and comparisons should be held down to few items. Don't ask respondents to compare ten to fifteen problems in the community.

9. Be careful about the use of open-ended questions and fixed format or closed-ended questions. Both kinds of questions have strengths, but they also have limitations. Closed-ended questions are easy to quantify but give only limited information. Open-ended questions provide more information but are very difficult to quantify. While the additional data may be rich in information and emotions, it also gives respondents the opportunity to introduce new variables that aren't under consideration. You will need to run an additional statistical analysis (i.e., content analysis) to use open-ended data appropriately. (Rubin & Rubin, 1986; Brueggemann, 1996)

10. Pilot or pretest questions at the outset. This allows you to check that the questions are eliciting the information you are after.

Sampling Techniques

There are stringent guidelines for selecting the sample to be used in the needs assessment survey. It really isn't feasible for practitioners to survey all residents of a given community. Therefore, practitioners must use scientific sampling procedures. If they carefully follow the guidelines of the sampling procedure selected, then N = 200, 500, or perhaps 1,000 respondents may be large enough to accurately reflect the opinions of the population.*

The goal of selecting a sample is to enable the practitioner to survey the people most directly affected by, or at least most vested in, the problem being studied. Once the appropriate population has been identified the practitioner seeks to get a representative sample of the affected group or groups. There are texts to help practitioners to determine appropriate sizes for survey samples. Remember that sample size must be large enough to represent the population under consideration and to enable the use of statistical analysis to evaluate and understand the data.

Basically four sampling techniques are used in needs assessments: simple random sampling, systematic sampling, stratified random sampling, and cluster sampling.

Simple random sampling isn't difficult and is nonetheless usually appropriate. It can be used with small samples because it can be as simple as putting the names of city directors in a hat and drawing out a third of them. Or the practitioner can enter everyone's name in a computer and then select the desired sample by using a random number system.

Systematic sampling is another way to obtain a random sample. The names of everyone in the population under study are generated into a single list. The practitioner then decides the percentage of the total population that will constitute the sample, and respondents are selected until that desired number is reached. The process begins with the first name being randomly selected from the list; then, from that point, every fifth, sixth, or tenth name (or names at some other regular interval) are chosen until the total sample is identified. It doesn't matter if the first name comes from the top of the list, the middle, or the end. The principle is that everyone has the same opportunity of being selected.

Perhaps the technique most often used by practitioners working in communities is *stratified random sampling*. The reason is that practitioners usually work in communities with significant diversity, and they must assure that there is appropriate representation of all groups. Stratification in this context means not only that the sample represents the entire population but that it is proportional and represents particular subgroups as well. A simple random sample will not guarantee proportional representation of subgroups because it is not designed to do so.

First, the practitioner needs to know the percentage of each subgroup in the population. The practitioner will then draw a random sample in which the various subgroups make up the same percentages. For example, if there are 18 percent Native Americans, 20 percent Hispanics, and 26 percent African

---

* N stands for the sample size.

Americans in the population, a stratified sample of 500 must contain 90 Native Americans, 100 Hispanics, 130 African Americans, and 180 respondents from the remaining part of the population.

Cluster sampling is a variation on stratified sampling. At times the population contains so many different groups that the practitioner can't survey all of them. The practitioner can, however, cluster people into categories determined by the purpose of the study. Once these clusters are identified, the practitioner can draw a stratified sample using the process described above. Examples of clustering criteria include religion, income, family size, age, occupation, and education.

It is essential that the community be surveyed in a way that recognizes both the purpose of the survey and the overall composition of the population. It makes little sense, for example, to use a simple random sample to study the role of racial tension in a local school district with, say, only 15 percent racial minorities. Whites are unlikely to see or report tension, division, discrimination, or oppression. A sample with too few minority respondents may produce an invalid conclusion that relations are fine when they are not.

Practitioners should include cover letters with surveys that are mailed out and should follow a script during telephone calls and person-to-person interviews. People need to know why the study is being conducted and what is intended to be accomplished with the data gathered. It is also important that the study be sanctioned. This can often be accomplished with a statement signed by key informants, power brokers, civic leaders, religious leaders, or public officials. Also, the practitioner should help respondents to understand how critical it is that they participate in the study. In some cases, the potential benefit of the study will affect respondents directly, and they must be aware of this. In other cases, the participants will receive no direct benefit from the study, but their friends, children, and other family members might. If this is so, practitioners should emphasize a mix of altruism and the interests of those close to the respondents.

Finally, it is only appropriate to indicate that there are some known limitations to needs assessment that need to be identified. Those limitations include: (1) Cost can be formidable; (2) Even though the study can be conducted with rigor and exactness, sample attrition and non-response rates of questionnaires may substantially negate the representativeness of an actual set of respondents. Perhaps the individuals we needed to hear from the most failed to respond; (3) Surveys invariably rely on self-report which assures a great degree of subjectivity on issues for which we need objective data; (4) Most surveys utilize closed-ended questions that are not as effective in exploring the causes of problems and their possible remedies. Too often the survey measures only the "symptoms" of the real problems. Thus, we are literally left with very little usable data (5) Attempts to assure representativeness through our sampling techniques don't always produce desired goals. Often the practitioner is dealing with transient populations or populations that often are not cooperative. There may be too much pain on their part and they may see nothing good coming from their participation (Meenaghan & Kilty, 1993).

ASSESSING SUPPORT AND FACILITATING CHANGE

Before we conclude this chapter, let's return once again to the issue of a support base for facilitating change. Remember, it is not enough to have good ideas and good causes. Other practitioners are out there trying to corner some of the community's scarce resources for their own constituencies. These colleagues also have legitimate concerns and believe that if their programs were financed, the community would be a better place to live. However, if the good ideas of these colleagues are funded, the vulnerable population with whom the practitioner works may lose even more ground. People experiencing the most discrimination and oppression are often the least popular causes and also have the greatest difficulty coming together on their own behalf.

For example, in a residential area of a large western city where drug manufacturing and distribution was very high, there was a huge "public outcry" at the death of a teenage boy as he crossed a major thoroughfare on his way to high school. Obviously, it was a tragedy and something about which all citizens should be concerned. However, the only response to the tragedy that the "concerned citizens" could agree on appeared to be the building of a million-dollar "pedestrian sky-walk" (an overpass). This group of good and caring people came together in a united front and kept the pressure on the state transportation agency and local elected officials until they had a commitment for the sky-walk. To show the energy, strength, and support of this group, literally hundreds of citizens stayed up all night and supported the workmen as they put the steel beams in place across the busy highway. Now let's step back a moment and contrast this group with the vulnerable population of the same neighborhood who were concerned about drugs but who felt helpless to address their problem. The point here is that the group who wanted the sky-walk knew about *positional* power, they made sure their concern was addressed. The people worried about drug distribution couldn't even organize themselves to action, so nothing constructive occurred.

Practitioners always have to consider power and how it can be brought into their practice. Among other things, they must recognize that the same people will not be helpful under all circumstances. Power brokers have their own special interests and emotionally charged concerns. At times, these concerns may conflict with the practitioner's current project. Practitioners can't assume they know where influentials will line up on any particular social issue. For example, Senator Orrin Hatch is thought to be very conservative in general, a number of times he and Senator Ted Kennedy have aligned themselves on important human service bills (child welfare services, mental health concerns, etc.). Though it is well established that Senator Hatch is a strong advocate for the mentally ill, it's only when people know him or talk to him that they learn why he has this concern. Because legislator's values stem from their life experiences, never presume to know how they will vote without examining their records or interviewing people who know them well. A fiscal conservative may be a resource on surprising issues and programs.

In short, practitioners need to know who in the community can be called on for support. Practitioners must appreciate that support may be a simple endorsement, active participation on a committee, or brokering for money. Practitioners must assess possible roles for different actors and groups and link these considerations to force field dynamics—driving and restraining forces and their potency, consistency, and amenability. These principles can be applied to influentials as well as to the situations needing change.

Securing Sanction

Another task the practitioner must complete is securing sanctions. Perhaps it is obvious by now, but working with individual power brokers and obtaining sanction to act are not the same thing. When practitioners plan activities they need to ascertain who must be approached and brought aboard to sponsor and provide legitimacy to their projects. For example, a practitioner may need the clergy of a neighborhood to step up and endorse a project. In essence, the clergy tell the neighborhood that the practitioner and project are okay, can be trusted, and should be supported. On other occasions, the sanctioning body may be found within the public electorate, major social service agencies, a large corporate entity, or a group of concerned citizens (perhaps an oppressed special population) who will come together in a unified front. The point is simply that most practitioners have no power without the sanction of some legitimizing body.

Assessing the Power of the Opposition

As important as understanding the base of support for a project is understanding the likely opposition—who it is, the source and nature of their power, and the strength of their power. Not all influentials will support an undertaking, and practitioners need to know who the opposition is and why they are not in favor of the project. Sometimes the reason is quite simple: for example, their own pet project is being initiated at the same time as the practitioner's. On other occasions they will oppose a project because of the long-term financial obligation it may impose on the community. Sophisticated power brokers know that projects initiated with outside "seed money" can end up costing someone at the local level enormous sums.

It is essential that the practitioner measure the strength of the opposition against the support and sanction for a project. If the opposition is too strong, the practitioner must reconsider the plan and reevaluate its feasibility.

Opposition is no reason to scuttle a project, but it does mean that the practitioner should revisit the details of the plan, timetables, and so forth. After such review the practitioner might find it wisest to delay the initiation of the plan and to do more public education, especially of community influentials. Another strategy is to form a coalition with other groups in the community who might then strengthen your power base.

It is not uncommon for social service agencies to join together around common issues and concerns. It can be particularly useful when private and public providers cooperate. For example, a number of agencies from both sectors may come together to develop a crisis line or offer a joint educational program. Such collaborative efforts, however, do not ensure that resulting benefits accrue equally to all.

Finally, because political and organizational resources may be linked it is also important to know the restraining forces and the opposition's possible tactics.

Identifying Linkage Possibilities: The Power of Coalitions

Cooperation is one of the most important strategies practitioners can master in working with communities. There are no hard and fast rules, but it is essential that practitioners learn how, when, and where to cooperate with other organizations and groups. Rarely can a practitioner take a system on alone; far more often a practitioner will need to negotiate a cooperative endeavor. This process is often called forming a coalition. Rubin and Rubin (1986), however, identify three different cooperative endeavors: cooperative efforts, coalitions, and alliances.

Cooperative efforts are a loose form of coordination. They occur when two or more groups with similar goals or plans coordinate their efforts for the common good of all participating groups. They do not involve anything as structured as a jointly developed agenda. For example, doctors, nurses, and social workers may all decide to support a particular piece of legislation regarding battered children rather than alternative bills. All three groups are concerned about children, and the efforts of all three groups reinforce each other; but each group continues to pursue its goal independently. Moreover, cooperative effort is simply "issue" linked and will end as soon as the legislative session ends.

Coalitions, by contrast, are generally formed to address long-term problems that are too big for one group to handle. In this situation, the group looks around for others with like interests to join in a cooperative endeavor around a joint agenda. When groups form a coalition they create a new layer of organization by establishing a steering committee with members from each of the participating groups. This committee is responsible for setting goals, negotiating differences, developing strategies, and so forth. Its members also take the major decisions, developed by the steering committee, back to their individual organizations for approval to act.

There are real pros and cons to entering into coalitions. A coalition is usually initiated by a party needing help with a particular problem. That group appears to have more to gain from cooperation, and thus the coalition may not benefit all parties equally. Therein lies the problem. While not formalized, there is an unwritten, unspoken understanding that the party being helped now will reciprocate by supporting the efforts of the other cooperating groups when called upon—and these other groups will not forget this "debt." There are serious drawbacks to this type of arrangement, especially when groups form coalitions with others whose overall goals may be incompatible with their own. Practitioners must be aware of the rules of the coalition game— they should not seek coalitions unless they are willing to reciprocate support and action on the behalf of the other coalition members.

We illustrate how coalitions can backfire with a scenario that occurred in a small rural state that needed federal agency assistance to develop services for AIDS victims. The Centers for Disease Control (CDC) in Atlanta were contacted and agreed to provide software and training for professionals who were tracking and counseling AIDS victims. In addition, physicians were provided special training at the CDC in the treatment of people with AIDS. Some time after the cooperative endeavor was completed, the cooperating staff at the CDC came back to the state and made a request that was completely unrelated to the purpose of the coalition. They sought permission to contact county coroners for data on suicide rates in the counties of the state. This was information the state had systematically refused to send to the CDC because of concern about damage to the state's image should the information be published. The state now found itself in a very difficult position. It was payback time, and the state didn't feel it could renege in good conscience. It instead negotiated a compromise position whereby it would provide the data but only with the understanding that the CDC wouldn't disseminate the statistics.

Another caution when working with coalitions has to do with knowing the individual actors. A practitioner needs to evaluate the interest and motivation of each person in the coalition. To whom do they owe their allegiance? For instance, when the "heat" is turned up, what forces and dynamics might influence them to back away, thus leaving the practitioner "high and dry?" It is important to understand the role of personal profiles and agenda, as well as the formal agenda over which they joined the practitioner's project.

The reasons for forming *alliances* can be quite similar to those for undertaking other cooperative endeavors, but the process is much more formal and structured. Alliances occur when a number of organizations come together around common concerns and maintain permanent, professional staff to represent them. Continuing negotiations among all alliance members over every issue are thus unnecessary. In most cases, the professional staff also provide technical assistance to member organizations. An example of this type of cooperative endeavor was introduced earlier when we talked about regional governmental organizations. It is not uncommon for rural counties and towns to form an alliance, or "association of governments," for the purpose of providing mental and public health care. They may also ally around water issues, waste disposal issues, and land use.

As we bring this chapter to a close, note how often we have referred to the generalist framework and to the problem-solving approach that guides practice. Not everything done in community practice corresponds point for point with the problem-solving process presented. Nonetheless, practitioners need to carefully identify and conceptualize problems before moving forward. In essence, practitioners must be "clear" about what data they are attempting to collect and why they are collecting it.

CONCLUSION

In this chapter we discussed the concept of community, as elusive amalgam of many dynamics. The practitioner must not enter into a community as if all communities of equal size, geography, and sociodemographic makeup are alike. To understand the personality and dynamics of a given community practitioners must complete their homework. This is a prerequisite for introducing any form of social change.

Entrance into a community necessitates a careful assessment of the many variables and idiosyncrasies that define the community. We presented various methods for conducting needs assessments. It is very difficult to introduce any change that is not viewed as necessary by a particular community, thus the importance of valid needs assessment. Finally, we discussed how to use support from others in facilitating community change.

CHAPTER 6

Cultivating Change

In America, the roots of community organization and practice are embedded in the Charity Organization Movement, Jane Addams's Hull House, and the Settlement House Movement of the turn of the century. Socially conscious men and women were uncanny in their ability to organize neighborhoods and to facilitate social action. With the possible exception of the civil rights movement of the 1960s and early 1970s, no other era in American history has experienced such significant social change. Since these early social movements, professional social workers have tried to organize their thinking and clearly articulate the conceptual foundation from which they work. This chapter will examine the methodology of community practice, organization, and practitioner responses.

APPROACHING COMMUNITY CHANGE

Before we move to the approaches and models currently used by practitioners working in larger systems, let us consider why social workers become involved in community practice, particularly because it is such a complicated process. Weil and Gamble identify seven purposes and issues associated with practitioner involvement in community organization:

1. Improving the quality of life of community residents
2. Advocating for community interests, especially those of populations at risk
3. Developing human social and economic strategies
4. Establishing service and program planning
5. Developing local, national, and international service integration and coordination
6. Establishing political and social action strategies
7. Engaging the community in the press for social justice (Beebe, Winchester, Edwards, et al., 1995)

A practitioner starting work in a larger system is taking on a complex entity that has 101 ways of assuring the failure of any project. Remember, large institutions and organizations do not change simply because a change would be good or because it appears to be the "right thing" to do. Systems theory contends that individuals, institutions, communities, and other living organisms dread disequilibrium. They enjoy the predictability of their current state. Disequilibrium means a potential loss of control and a feeling of craziness, even within large organizations. Systems in disequilibrium will scramble to return to a previous state even when it is not in their best interest. It takes considerable time for organizations to establish their power bases; thus any suggestion of change causes, almost by instinct, defensiveness or restraint.

The suggestion that an organization join with others to improve its power base often meets with a certain amount of skepticism. While improving position and obtaining additional power will always be regarded with at least some degree of favor, there are clearly times when the gains of becoming stronger do not outweigh the liabilities. Therefore, the practitioner should anticipate that an organization might perceive its power base as being diluted or dismantled if it joins with other organizations. Large organizations typically try to strengthen their positions through internal reorganization and redefinition of task or mission.

Under normal conditions, large organizations will join together only to improve their power bases or to avoid extinction. Organizations sometimes lose their viability; at that point they are willing to join with other organizations in order to survive. Conversely, some organizations will attempt even hostile takeovers in order to improve their power bases or corner particular markets. Private organizations and businesses use this tactic, but large agencies and human service organizations will often instead attempt to improve their power bases and obtain additional resources by repositioning themselves.

In considering the models of community practice, it is important not to become dismayed at their similarities. They are conceptual guides intended to focus professional activity, bring structure to the practitioner's work, and stimulate the critical thinking needed to be successful. One model may look much like another, but each has its own discriminating features. Figure 1, compiled by Weil and Gamble, will prove very helpful if the reader takes the time to review the five defining criteria listed by the authors. Remember too, at times best practice demands that practitioners combine models to adapt to a specific project.

For years, the work of Jack Rothman (1967; cited in Weil, 1966) provided the standard practice framework for community organizers. His seminal article, which identified the three models of social planning, locality development, and social action, still serves as the standard for determining macropractice tactics and strategies. Though others introduced elaborations and variations of these models, the original three stand as the generally accepted organizing models of community practice. Marie Weil (1996) offers a concise summary of the principal constructs of Rothman's three models:

> *Locality development model*—"Locality development had major process goals of self-help and community capacity building and focused on broad groups of people involved in determining and solving their own problems. This model usually focused on a small community with citizens participating in an interactional problem solving process. The practitioner role was primarily that of enabler-catalyst, coordinator and teacher of problem solving skills" (Weil, 1996). *"Let's all get together and talk this over."*
>
> *Social planning model*—"Rothman's codification of the elements in social planning identified the major goals as problem solving focus on substantive community problems utilizing a basic change strategy of fact gathering and rational decision making for a total community or a specified functional community. The practitioner roles emphasized technical skills in research, analysis, program implementation and facilitation. The client role was typically expected to be consumer or recipient" (Weil, 1996). *"Let's get the facts and think through the logical next steps."*
>
> *Social action model*—"Rothman summarizes the elements of this model as including both task and process goals geared toward changing power relationships and basic institutions. Members of disadvantaged populations are the constituents of such groups with the practitioner functioning primarily as an activist advocate. Major strategies include contest or conflict to achieve goals" (Weil, 1996). *"Let's organize to overpower our oppressor and change the system."*

While Weil has done a nice job of summarizing Rothman's models, carefully review figure 2, a table taken from Rothman's 1967 article. This table separates primary concepts and views them through each practice mode. It is inclusive enough that it indicates to the practitioner a fairly clear approach to each particular community problem.

In order to better understand the notions driving Rothman's work, it is helpful to consider two other important concepts. Rothman (1964) and Gilbert and Specht (1977) identify what they refer to as the two modes, or levels, of community practice: these are *task* and *process,* and each has its own unique goals. Task goals are primarily the completion of concrete activities or the solution of delimited community problems. In essence, task is directed toward solving the currently identified functional problems of the system. Process goals, on the other hand, are directed toward strengthening and maintaining the community's ability to function over time. Process focuses on systems maintenance, enhancement, and empowerment (Rothman et al., 1995)

Practitioners know that any time they work with a client system, they

Figure 1 Current Models of Community Practice for Social Work

Comparative Characteristics	Neighborhood and Community Organizing	Organizing Functional Communities	Community Social and Economic Development	Social Planning	Program Development and Community Liaison	Political and Social Action	Coalitions	Social Movements
Desired outcome	Develop capacity of members to organize; change the impact of citywide planning and external development	Action for social justice focused on advocacy and on changing behaviors and attitudes; may also provide service	Initiate development plans from a grassroots perspective; prepare citizens to make use of social and economic investments	Citywide or regional proposals for action by elected body or human services planning councils	Expansion or redirection of agency program to improve community service effectiveness; organize new service	Action for social justice focused on changing policy or policy makers	Build a multi-organizational power base large enough to influence program direction or draw down resources	Action for social justice that provides a new paradigm for a particular population group or issue
System targeted or charge	Municipal government; external developers; community members	General public; government institutions	Banks; foundations; external developers; community citizens	Perspectives of community leaders; perspectives of human services leaders	Funders of agency programs; beneficiaries of agency services	Voting public; elected officials; inactived potential participants	Elected officials; foundations; government institutions	General public; political systems
Primary constituency	Residents of neighborhood, parish, or rural county	Like-minded people in a community, region, nation, or across the globe	Low-income marginalized, or oppressed population groups in a city or region	Elected officials: social agencies and interagency organizations	Agency board or administrators; community representatives	Citizens in a particular political jurisdiction	Organizations that have a stake in the particular issue	Leaders and organizations able to create new visions and images

Figure 1 Current Models of Community Practice for Social Work—(Continued)

Comparative Characteristics	Model							
	Neighborhood and Community Organizing	Organizing Functional Communities	Community Social and Economic Development	Social Planning	Program Development and Community Liaison	Political and Social Action	Coalitions	Social Movements
Scope of concern	Quality of life in the geographic area	Advocacy for particular issue or population	Income, resource, and social support development; improved basic education and leadership skills	Integration of social needs into geographic planning in public arena; human services network coordination	Service development for a specific population	Building political power; institutional change	Specified issue related to social need or concern	Social justice within society
Social work roles	Organizer Teacher Coach Facilitator	Organizer Advocate Writer communicator Facilitator	Negotiator Promoter Teacher Planners Manager	Researcher Proposal writer Communicator Manager	Spokesperson Planner Manager Proposal writer	Advocate Organizer Researcher Candidate	Mediator Negotiator Spokesperson	Advocate Facilitator

Weil, M. & Gamble, D. (1995) "Community Practice Models," *Encyclopedia of Social Work*, 9th Edition, pp. 577–594; *Journal of Community Practices*, Volume 3, Nos. 3/4 (1996), pp. 43–44. Reprinted by permission of author.

Figure 2   Three Community Intervention Approaches According to Selected Practice Variables

	Mode A (Locality Development)	Mode B (Social Planning Policy)	Mode C (Social Action)
1. Goal categories of community action	Community capacity and integration; self-help (process goals)	Problem solving with regard to substantive community problems (task goals)	Shifting of power relationships and resources; basic institutional change (task of process goals)
2. Assumptions concerning community structure and problem conditions	Community eclipsed, anomie; lack of relationships and demographic problem-solving capacities; static tradional community	Substantive social problems, mental and physical health, housing, recreation, etc.	Aggrieved populations, social injustice, deprivation, inequality
3. Basic change strategy	Involving a broad cross section of people in determining and solving their own problems	Gathering data about problems and making decisions on the most logical course of action	Crystalizing issues and mobilizing people to take action against enemy targets
4. Characteristic change tactics and techniques	Consensus: communication among community groups and interests; group discussion	Consensus or conflict	Conflict confrontation, direct action, negotiation
5. Salient practitioner roles	Enabler-catalyst, coordinator; teacher of problem-solving skills and ethical values	Fact gatherer and analyst, program implementer, expediter	Activist advocate; agitator, broker, negotiator, partisan
6. Medium of change	Guiding small, task-oriented groups	Guiding formal organizations and treating data	Guiding mass organizations and political processes

must attend to the cognitive, affective, and behavioral aspects of that client. As when working with individuals, task behavior involves cognitive functioning. In essence, the pursuit of task goals is a cognitive activity. The pursuit of process goals, on the other hand, is an affective activity. Process involves the feelings, emotions, and well-being of the community. Rothman and Gilbert and Specht see locality development as emphasizing process (affective) goals. Social planning clearly focuses on task (cognitive) goals; it emphasizes problem solving with the required skills of research, analysis, and systematic and reasoned action. Social action can be either task or process. Social action planning goals

Figure 2   Three Community Intervention Approaches According to Selected Practice Variables—*(Continued)*

	Mode A (Locality Development)	Mode B (Social Planning Policy)	Mode C (Social Action)
7. Orientation toward power structure(s)	Members of power structure as collaborators in a common venture	Power structure as employers and sponsors	Power structure as external larger of action: oppressors to be coerced or overturned
8. Boundary definition of the beneficiary system	Total geographic community	Total community or community segment	Community segment
9. Assumptions regarding interests of community subparts	Common interests or reconciliable differences	Interests reconciliable or in conflict	Conflicting interests which are not easily reconciliable, scarce resources
10. Conception of beneficiaries	Citizens	Consumers	Victims
11. Conception of beneficiary role	Participants in an interactional problem-solving process	Consumers or recipients	Employers, constituents, members
12. Use of Empowerment	Building the capacity of a community to make collaborative and informed decisions; promoting feeling of personal mastery by residents	Finding out from consumers about their needs for service; informing consumers of their service choices	Achieving objective power for beneficiary system–the right and means to impact community decisions; promoting a feeling of mastery by participants

Rothman (1995). Reprinted by permission of F. E. Peacock, Inc.

focus on task; however, social action goals, overall, are also heavy on affect or process. No community action activity is unemotional or bland. The whole process of social action can spark emotional reactions and stir deep feelings.

The change tactics of locality development depend on open discussion, communication, and consensus as a way to solve problems. Social planning uses fact finding and analytical skills and both consensus and conflict resolution. Not surprisingly, given Weil's description, social action sometimes uses a militant advocacy modality that emphasizes confrontation and direct action (Rothman et al., 1995).

Two other considerations should be reviewed before we move on: the *role of the practitioner* and the *role of the intended beneficiaries* in each of these models. The role of the practitioner varies widely. The professional role of the social worker in locality development is "enabler" or "encourager," while the role in social planning is "expert" with extensive professional training. By contrast, the role in social action is not necessarily a continuing one: it is primarily "organizer" and catalyst. Having gotten a group of people going, the practitioner is sometimes left with very little influence. The community group, thus motivated, may have little need of the practitioner. Indeed, once empowered, the group may be unwilling to take any further advice from the practitioner. Some social workers are genuinely surprised when they find themselves unable to rein in these groups' activities (Rothman et al., 1995).

In social planning the role of beneficiaries is rather passive. While the method is rigorous for the practitioner, clients simply are consumers or recipients of the new services. Locality development is much more active for beneficiaries. While the community members are guided in their problem solving, they are nevertheless involved in self-help activities. Social action is the most empowering model for beneficiaries. However, it can be problematic for the practitioner because the action group may reach a point at which it no longer cooperates with those who helped to organize it.

Rothman suggests that in the social action model the practitioner's employer could be among the beneficiaries (Rothman et al., 1995). While this may sound strange, the fact of the matter is that it happens all the time as clients "make waves," necessitating positive change in the practitioner's organization. Something as simple as a group of mental health workers refusing to visit clients in marked state cars may result in greater recognition of the dignity and intrinsic worth of the mentally ill client or a more caring, sensitive mental health center. The formation of a "food coalition" by a group of low-income citizens may result in broadened services in a more viable and visible community action agency. The result of such action is win-win because the clients benefit and so does the community agency.

A third important consideration, now receiving much attention in the literature, is the impact of community practice models on *women*. The traditional models of community practice have been characterized as fitting male gender stereotypes and not addressing feminist issues and roles. Weis (1995; cited in Weil, 1996) identifies eight feminist principles to consider:

1. Feminists will always act to support female values and processes.
2. Feminists place great value on process and the product that comes from process.
3. Feminists are committed to consciousness-raising processes.
4. Feminists affirm the variety and diversity of women's experiences while working for wholeness and unity.

5. Feminists work toward the empowerment of women through the reconceptualization of power and empowerment.

6. Feminists seek the empowerment of women through democratic structuring of organizations and systems.

7. Feminists organize and become political in their attempts to achieve collective solutions to oppressive situations.

8. Feminists organize to bring about structural change in organizations, institutions, and other societal structures that oppress through sexism, racism, and so forth.

In 1987, Ruth Brandwein asserted the need to use androgyny, wholism, synergy, a win-win power orientation, webs of relations, and egalitarian relations as the prism through which to view community organization activity. In essence, we are being challenged to view women as capable, competent actors and not simply as objects to be acted upon. Most traditional community models are thought to be so steeped in male gender stereotypes that practitioners must exercise constant vigilance to bring about constructive corrections. Courses of action that facilitate the self-awareness and empowerment of women are essential to all practice activities.

A fourth consideration in community practice is the omnipresence of powerful dynamics associated with *cultural, racial, and ethnic diversity*. In the needs assessment section of chapter 5 we cautioned readers to be sensitive to the dynamics of diversity. Recognizing the universal importance of diversity, Rivera and Erlich recommend that practitioners approach all community organization activities by considering the following:

> 1) similar cultural and racial identifications; 2) familiarity with customs and traditions, etc.; 3) intimate knowledge of language and sub-group slang; 4) knowledge of leadership styles and development; 5) an analytical framework for political and economic analysis; 6) knowledge of past organizing strategies—strengths and limitations; 7) skills in conscientization and empowerment; 8) skills in assessing community psychology; 9) knowledge of organizational behavior; 10) skills in evaluative and participatory research; 11) skill in program planning, development and administration; and 12) an awareness of self and personal strengths and limitations. (quoted in Weil, 1996)

It is not possible to be an expert on all racial and cultural groups, but practitioners can learn to discipline themselves to be sensitive to the concerns that diverse people bring to the table. Because practitioners obviously cannot fake an understanding of a particular culture, they must be comfortable asking diverse groups to help them to know, see, and feel the group's fears, hurts, and hopes for the future.

New models are constantly being added to those proposed by Rothman. In order to keep abreast of changes in society, macropractice must always be subject to new thinking and conceptualization. Weil and Gamble have conducted an extensive review of the literature and identified eight models of community practice, including revisions of the three basic Rothman models:

1. *Neighborhood and community organizing*—The central purpose of this model is to "develop the capacity of [community] members to organize effectively, develop appropriate strategies, and build power and influence to achieve desired goals in their social, political, economic, and physical environment." The practitioner assists residents of local areas as they address quality-of-life issues. The practitioner is an organizer, teacher, coach, and facilitator. Residents learn to identify issues, set goals, determine change strategies, implement their plan, and evaluate their strategies. This model focuses on local control and empowerment of local residents to act in their own interest. *The primary functions, processes, and purposes of this model are those activities associated with* organizing *groups to act* (Weil, 1996).

2. *Organizing functional communities*—This model also has as its major focus the organizing of like-minded citizens to advocate for issues specific to the community. The central purpose is to organize functional groups—from among the general public, select institutions, and so forth—to advocate for social justice through the changing of policies, behaviors, and attitudes. The practitioner is an organizer, advocate, communicator, and facilitator. Education of the public and advocacy of the identified issues are the primary strategies. *The primary functions, processes, and purposes of this model are also those of organizing like-minded citizens to act. The emphasis is on education of the general public* (Weil, 1996).

3. *Community social and economic development*—This model merges social and economic development. The central purpose is social justice and focuses on the "development of people, their capacities and skills, so that they can initiate and maintain grassroots plans and projects, improve their social and economic conditions, and support and sustain their home environment and its resources" (Weil, 1996). It emphasizes the empowerment of low-income residents, the marginalized, and oppressed groups. The impetus for change flows from the grassroots, and thus the citizens must be prepared and involved. The practitioner is a planner, teacher, manager, promoter, and negotiator. *The primary functions, processes and purposes of this model are those associated with the* development *of programs and projects* (Weil, 1996).

4. *Social planning*—Social planning takes place at both local and regional levels and primarily involves elected officials and human service agencies. It is a model involving the participation of experts and is mostly carried on by "others" on behalf of those needing services. Social planning

includes the classic rational planning models grounded in specialized expertise and research and data, and it places strong emphasis on rational decision making. While some social workers are uncomfortable with the model's stress on "expertise," in its pure form it is still a model of influentials doing things for their constituencies. The practitioner will often be regarded as an expert by virtue of professional training, and for this reason the practitioner may eventually become a community influential. The practitioner is a promoter, teacher, planner, negotiator, and manager. *The primary functions, processes, and purposes of this model are those associated with all the dynamics of very carefully and rigorously conceptualized and articulated* planning (Weil, 1996)

5. *Program development and community liaison*—The purpose of this model is the creation of a new service or the expansion or redirection of an agency program to improve responsiveness to community needs. It encourages the active involvement of clients, staff, and other interested citizens in needs assessment and program planning. In the process that takes place, a particular agency targets itself for change and then liaisons with clients and other agencies regarding the needed change. The agencies that join in these liaisons and developmental activities are not usually devoted to "community practice" but rather to "direct" services. The significance of this model is its emphasis on mutual planning strategies involving community members, its bringing together of clients and interested citizens with agencies providing services. The practitioner is a planner, manager, proposal writer, and spokesperson. *The primary functions, processes, and purposes of this model are those associated with all the dynamics of expanding and redirecting existing agency functions and planning new services* (Weil, 1996).

6. *Political and social action*—This model targets public elected officials and others who are involved with social policy. It is understood that social policy must be influenced in order to achieve social justice. The practitioner helps citizens to pursue social justice by focusing on changing policy or policymakers or on changing the actions of corporations that put low-income groups at a disadvantage. The overall focus of the model is on political power and influencing and balancing that power. The practitioner empowers citizens and encourages them to take action. The practitioner is an advocate, organizer, researcher, and candidate. *The primary functions, processes, and purposes of this model are directed to* change (Weil, 1996).

7. *Coalitions*—Coalitions allow agencies to improve their power bases while retaining their autonomy. Coalitions are used primarily to build multiorganizational power bases large enough to influence the direction of social programs or effectively demand resources that can be used in the common

interests of the coalition. Coalitions occur when agencies have a stake in a particular issue and want to influence elected officials, foundations, governments, or institutions. The organizations' motives are rarely altruistic. The practitioner is a mediator, negotiator, and spokesperson. *The primary functions, processes, and purposes of this model are directed to* change (Weil, 1996).

8. *Social movements*—Social movements are beyond the purview of social work per se. While practitioners often become active participants in social movements, the movements themselves are much bigger than the profession. The targets for change are the general public and political systems. In some cases legislative considerations are involved. Social movements are seldom if ever begun or directed exclusively by professional organizers. They are successful only if they receive grassroots support and grow beyond an identification with one person or organization. "As a social movement succeeds, the ideals that it has advanced are accepted as new, legitimized political and social norms." The practitioner is a facilitator and advocate, for the most part providing behind-the-scenes support and influence. *The primary functions, processes, and purposes of this model are directed once again to* change (Weil, 1996).

These eight models have many similarities and many differences. Often the practitioner will have to think through the implications of each approach before choosing one. In many of the models, the practitioner has the delicate task of moving into and out of leadership roles. On some occasions the practitioner takes a back seat to indigenous leaders; on others the practitioner is at the center of the action. Because roles vary so much, practitioners must focus on the knowledge and skills they must possess in small group dynamics, leadership, committee work, and interagency activity—topics discussed throughout this book.

In concluding this section we must warn the reader about a self-defeating trap that may seem to have been laid by the section's discussion. That trap has to do with power, influentials, elites, and decision makers. Many of the models suggest that a practitioner who cannot mobilize their support, or at least neutralize their negative influence, cannot succeed as a community organizer. The implication is that practitioners are impotent to effect change on their own. While there is some practical wisdom in the suggestion that practitioners have limited influence without help from others, it is not a "done deal," nor does social determinism come into play. History fortunately records the successes of Jane Addams and others to remind us that the "one" still has a role in social change. The contemporary work of Professor Yunus in India, where he focused on the poor, and women in particular, to bring about economic and social change, is just one example of one person's ability to bring about change.

USING KEY INFORMANTS

We have outlined a number of theories and constructs associated with power and its many facets. It is now useful to discuss some of the practical realities faced by powerful people.

Those in power who are decision makers and influentials occupy their positions largely because of demonstrated ability and successful performance. A corollary is also worth noting: lack of ability and poor performance can cause people to lose their positions. Large organizations, institutions, and political bodies typically succeed if their leadership performs well. Thus, when key decision makers are approached about activities that may affect their organizations, they will immediately anticipate the impact of the proposal not only on the organizations they represent but on themselves as well. A key decision maker involved in a project that goes awry is in a position to take considerable heat. Yet the practitioner may have difficulty uncovering these fears because the decision maker may not be totally honest with the practitioner. Leaders can avoid supporting a project simply by "going by the book"—in other words, giving organizational reasons for saying no rather than being honest about their personal fears. Practitioners must anticipate and plan to resolve or neutralize any and all leader or organizational losses before they make their first approach. They can do this by asking colleagues or other key community informants what they believe the leader being approached may fear and what she or he stands to lose by signing on to the project.

What we're suggesting is simply that institutions and organizations can go into a self-protection mode the moment they hear of changes that might affect them. Remember, the introduction of a much needed service can reflect badly on an existing agency that hasn't responded to the need. Moreover, political leaders and other power brokers often steer clear of situations that provide no immediate or ultimate gain for them. In other words, the project and population to be served may not be such that the potential "political gain" warrants the support of the influentials. For example, a neighborhood may have a substantial number of residents diagnosed as HIV positive. It may seem only prudent for the community and its power brokers to develop respite services for them. Yet the community may be denying the magnitude of the problem (maybe for moral reasons), and thus the political leaders and other influentials may refuse to embrace any such proposal. Another example illustrates how a new program can make an existing agency look bad. Suppose a proposal has been put together for the local mental health center to hire someone who can work effectively with "dual diagnosis" and "borderline" clients. Center staff may want to support this service because they are frustrated and worn out from working with these populations. The center's director, however, may fight the proposal because he or she knows the center's authority board (made up of elected officials) will ask why the center isn't already adequately serving this clientele since they meet the agency's criteria for care. Indeed, the board doesn't really care if the professional staff is burned out. As elected officials they must account to their constituency for keeping staff levels to a minimum. The political liabilities of the proposal may be too great for them to support it.

UNDERSTANDING WHY LEADERS DISLIKE BOARDS AND COMMITTEES

Now let's turn our attention to the role of boards and committees. There are unspoken attitudes and assumptions that practitioners need to know about in order to be successful in working with these groups. Directors and key decision makers of institutions and organizations are often not fond of working with boards and committees. Social workers, by contrast, have an extremely strong belief in the value and power of groups to facilitate change. Practitioners, in fact, can come into conflict with large institutions and their executive members around such issues as the partializing of authority and ultimate responsibility for task competition, the value of group activity (boards and committees) in relation to the development and execution of particular plans, and the sharing of authority between key people and the organization's administration.

Many power brokers and executive directors are cautious about group influence and find committees and boards nettlesome and even dysfunctional. They view such groups as impotent, incapable of any substantive work, and indeed as slowing down any process in which they are involved. Directors may refer to them as "do-nothing groups." The perception, put simply, is that far too many committees and boards "spin their wheels," make extra work for executives, needlessly prolong the development and ultimate execution of plans, stonewall organizational agenda, vie for power, and, finally, assume no responsibility for the success or failure of the plans they develop. In the face of these beliefs directors are often asked to give up to these groups some, if not all, of their authority to plan a particular project, and yet they can't give up the responsibility for the decisions made and their ultimate outcomes. Organization leaders typically want both responsibility and the authority before they move forward. They understand the "corporate rules": their heads are on the line in terms of the outcome of all decisions made within their organizations, yet in working with boards or committees, they see themselves as trying to carry out someone else's plan—there is nothing they fear more.

A particular major group that drives power brokers crazy is policy-making boards and committees. These groups may simply be advisory, or they may have real policy-making authority. In some ways the dynamics of the two groups are similar, but there is one very important difference. Advisory boards are just that; they offer advice to the organization that can then be accepted or rejected. Boards with policy-making authority, by contrast, can ultimately direct the activities of the organization. Both kinds of groups require careful treatment, however. Advisory boards, while they have no real authority, often behave as if they do. If the organization does not follow their suggestions, it must be prepared to deal with the consequences, among which is role confusion. Policy-making boards, not surprisingly, can cause real heartburn for executives and other administrative personnel because they can legitimately stop the organization from moving in a desired direction. When this happens the powerful people in the organization are diminished. Administrators and decision makers become far too vulnerable to the caprices of the board and even of individual board members.

We don't mean to be cynical or obsessed with power. Our point is that practitioners can't be naive about the real world. They must understand that there are always reasons for the way people and organizations behave. All behavior is meaningful. Agencies, organizations, and institutions are created for a purpose, and it behooves them to stay viable, on the cutting edge, and worthy of continued community support. Knowing this helps practitioners to see why an organization might support practitioner efforts on some occasions and resist them on others. Survival as a motivating force cannot be overestimated.

A community agency, for example, may resist a practitioner's efforts to pull it into a coalition or some other cooperative endeavor because it fears its weaknesses will be exposed Perhaps the agency isn't doing a good job of fulfilling the charge given it by the community, and it is afraid that the group will discover its omissions. This resistance is no reason for the practitioner to back away; the practitioner may simply need to help agency leaders to see the potential gains from joining the coalition rather than just the dangers. Having figured out the source of resistance, the practitioner may be able to show the vulnerable executives that working together, they can keep negative attention off the agency. This kind of relation is founded on trust, and it can only be built by working with colleagues in a professional manner and by respecting their dignity, value, and worth. Practitioners cannot be backbiters, supercritics, or badmouthers and still expect to have a collegial base of support. Colleagues and other influentials will approach the practitioner predicated on the way the practitioner treats others and interacts with the community. Since influentials talk to each other, the practitioner must strive always to show professionalism, integrity, honesty, trust, fairness, and respect for others. One bad decision, one unethical or questionable act, can sully the practitioner's reputation indefinitely. Simple principles always apply: The end doesn't justify the means. Don't use people. Value the contributions of others. Be ready to lend a helping hand.

SELECTING BOARD AND COMMITTEE MEMBERS

We now must discuss some selected group dynamics, as they relate to change. In particular, practitioners must learn how to choose members for a committee or board and how many people should be named to these groups.

It may even be necessary for practitioners to unlearn some things in order to make appropriate committee and board selections. For example, it is common sense to identify notables, power brokers, and influentials from the community to invite onto committees or boards. Indeed, practitioners are taught that it is critical to be able to identify the power brokers and decision makers of a neighborhood or community. It is not a good idea, however, to automatically invite all these people onto a committee or board. The wise course is to ask three or four of these decision makers to join; their presence gives the project credibility and implies to the community that it is worth supporting. In essence, they lend their names and credentials.

Why then only three or four of these people? The question itself suggest the answer. High-profile people and people with clout are sought by many groups, and as a result they are often overextended. We all know the advice: If you want to get a job done, give it to a busy person. While this has an element of truth, what happens too often is that these busy people, though very supportive of the practitioner and the project, are simply spread too thin. They miss meetings, participate little, and offer little tangible support. Therefore, when group members are being selected, it is useful to include capable "worker bees" who will go in and do the job. These people are not necessarily total unknowns, but they are not the heavy hitters. These committed workers are often drawn from among young professionals who are in the process of establishing themselves and gaining name recognition. They want to work. They want to be part of successful projects. In addition to their altruism, there's something in it for them if they do a good job.

Let's return to the topic of group composition. It is important to have, within a committee or board, representatives from the group affected by the proposed plan. This is a precaution against overloading with power brokers. People can be influential even if they are not members of the "in" crowd of community leaders. They are influential because they are respected and trusted by the constituency being served. These people are often referred to as indigenous leaders. By including such leaders practitioners are serving an important human principle: people must be actively involved in all projects capable of affecting them. All groups, but especially populations at risk, are offended when others presume to "do" for them. Such paternalism is demeaning, and it destroys the human spirit. Self-determination, empowerment, and self-respect are key healing concepts of the social work profession. People need to be primarily "actors" and not simply objects "acted upon." They deserve to be recognized as possessing dignity, value, and inherent worth. People and groups all have hopes, dreams, life experience, and a wealth of knowledge about real life and its impact on them. Practitioners must do everything possible to access these potential contributions.

Heterogeneity is another important consideration in the selection of group members. Diversity produces energy. Groups that are too homogeneous have difficulty getting "untracked." The group members can have so much in common, think so much alike, and view life so much alike that they reinforce each other's perceptions that change is not possible or even desirable. Furthermore, group members who are too much alike may fail to stimulate new ideas, explore new ways of thinking, or generate the necessary level of conflict. Heterogeneity conflict can provide energy with which to build.

Group size is also an important factor in committee selection. Aphorisms abound to the effect that "more is better," that many hands make light work." This may be sage advice when the task is harvesting crops or cleaning up a neighborhood (once the project is under way); it should not, however, determine group size. Excessively large groups are slow, cumbersome, and ineffective. Typically a few people do most of the work—for a variety of reasons, including people's tendency to assume that someone else will get the job done.

In 1954 Thelen introduced "the principle of least group size," which recommends that a group be as small as it can be and still accomplish the task. He talked about having all the achievement (content resources) and socialization (group process) skills required for the activity (task) at hand. In practice-related language, this means that practitioners should have only as many group members (probably seven or nine people but not more than twelve) needed to fulfill both the task and the group-building and maintenance roles crucial to group success (these roles are discussed in chapter 7).

Practitioners need both people who will maintain the group and bring fellow members along and people with the expertise necessary to be successful. Committee and board members are often called "resources." That means exactly what it seems to. Practitioners have to identify people who are expert in areas critical to the group and knowledgeable about the things the group is trying to accomplish. It doesn't matter how well meaning a group is if it doesn't have the knowledge, information, and expertise it needs to succeed. Without the right resources practitioners will find themselves in situations where neither efficiency nor effectiveness is evident.

Thelen's work also illuminates the dynamics underlying participation on community committees and boards. For example, he claimed that group members only remain motivated if they 1) are assured they are necessary to the group, 2) have an opportunity to grow while serving with the group (each member determines what constitutes growth—it's highly subjective), and 3) feel secure enough to carry out their responsibilities. The bottom line is for participants to feel that the group needs them, that they have something to contribute, and that they are respected for their ideas and work. Remember, feeling of service is a personal gain, even if that is not the conscious motivation.

Thelen offered specific reasons for groups to be kept as small as possible. As group size grows, he suggested, the following dynamics emerge (these dynamics intensify with each member added beyond twelve):

1. Each person has less time to test her or his ideals directly through overt participation.

2. Group members feel less pressure to participate, and the fact of one's non-participation is less visible.

3. Members experience more difficulty in expressing intimate thoughts and feelings (being real).

4. Members are more likely to "sit tight" and let someone else do the job.

5. Each member's influence, either positive or negative, on group thinking is lessened.

6. Members feel less responsible for meeting the demands of the group's task.

In large groups it is impossible for everyone to get equal "air" time. Instead, a few "top participants" do most of the talking (Bales, cited in Olmsted, 1955). When this occurs, very quickly norms fall into place governing who speaks, how much they say, what kind of information and comments have value, and so forth.

The selection of committee or board members can be critical to a practitioner's success or failure on a significant project. Most projects worth doing are difficult enough without wasting energy on problems rooted in group dynamics.

In sum, practitioners need to know why they are selecting particular people to participate on committees and boards. Groups that are too large quickly become unwieldy, so practitioners must think through carefully what expertise and knowledge on the part of group members will maximize the chances of success.

RESOLVING CONFLICT

Conflict is one of those processes that produces great discomfort. Many people have been taught to keep conflict out of their relations and lives, that it is very negative and only serves to fracture and divide. The essence of conflict is simply "difference." Conflict can be a source of energy for practitioners working with groups. It only becomes problematic as volatile emotions come into play and wrest the process from the practitioner's control. Practice suggests that good discussion is born in conflict and thrives on conflict, but the conflict must be one of ideas rather than personalities.

It isn't enough to say that practitioners and groups need conflict. It also isn't helpful to say, Deal with conflict as it arises. Practitioners need reliable ways to resolve conflict so that having harvested its energy, the group can move forward in it tasks, and also maintain its cohesion. Just how can practitioners work with groups in order to resolve conflict? Konopka (1972) identifies six types of conflict resolution:

1. *Withdrawal* is the exit of one part of the group—not physically, but in terms of participation. Every child knows about this type of conflict res-

olution. "Things aren't going my way, so I'm going to take my ball and go home." Some would say that this approach doesn't really resolve the issue, but we suggest it does for those who withdraw.

2. *Subjugation* is the willful silencing of one part of the group by another. It is achieved through the use of power, position, and numbers and can include violence, threats and ridicule. Subjugation was evident during the civil rights movement, and it is at work throughout the world today, in Ireland, Bosnia, and Africa, for example. Simply put, those in power impose their will on the powerless. The power used can flow from money status, position, or sheer numbers. Whatever the source, the powerful subgroup has the ability to control subjugated members.

3. *Majority rule,* or the "American way" is a form of subjugation. Though not arbitrary, it nonetheless involves one subgroup imposing its will on another—in this case, through a vote. This type of resolution is normally used because it is thought to be fast and expedient. In fact it can be slower because it invites resistance. The group members voted down are left wondering why they should support the majority decision when their concerns and points of view were discarded.

4. *Minority consent to majority rule* is a fairly high level process of conflict resolution. It is not subjugation because the minority after careful delib-eration *concedes* to the majority on a particular issue. However, care must be taken that it is not always the same subgroup doing the conceding. There must be give-and-take in this process. For example, a group may have members who represent a specific racial minority. As planning and discussion take place the practitioner must be careful that the racial minority is not always asked to modify its position.

5. *Compromise,* a high-level form of conflict resolution, occurs when neither side gets full satisfaction but each side agrees to the limits set on its own suggestions. Although it is not synonymous with *consensus,* the two terms are often used interchangeably. In consensus and compromise, everyone gets a say as the topic is discussed until the group agrees to move forward. The process—which may involve a lot of tension, conflict, and discom-fort—appears to be time consuming, but in fact, it can resolve conflict more quickly than majority rule because the group doesn't have to keep "paying" for the feelings of subjugated group members. Some view compromise as a loss for both parties because they give up something and, as a consequence, the result is not the "most desirable" to anyone. Consensus involves a syn-ergy whose win-win result is greater than the sum of its parts. As groups become larger they often move from small group process predicated on principles of consensus (everyone has a say, yet no one fully gets their way) to majority rule (subjugation of the minority by the majority). Clearly, when this happens—given the relation between ownership and responsi-bility—many group members are not part of what is developed.

6. *Integration* is a rare and highly complicated form of conflict resolution. It requires that each side desire to reach a common decision and be prepared to accept that decision even if it is quite different from what was originally proposed. All group members, Konopka asserts, must be willing and personally able to resolve their own feelings of "winning" or "losing" in relation to the final decision made. For example, Quakers are required to sit in silence for a period after group decisions are made so that they can work through any need to claim "victory" in the community decision.

Konopka warns group leaders about unwittingly using processes that assure failure. Failure manifests itself in failed projects but also possibly in the practitioner's loss of influence. Practitioners have to remember that they are only as successful as the groups they work with. Practitioners who work successfully with boards and committees are in high demand. Their reputation and influence flow naturally from their performance. Unfortunately, we are far too prone to do everything the "American way," which means majority rule. A review of Konopka's classification, however, shows that this is not always the best type of conflict resolution. The people practitioners work with have often been the "target" of this kind of problem solving. If they feel subjugated or used, they may "stonewall," keeping the group from moving forward, even though it has reached a decision.

More often than not the projects with which practitioners are involved affect and are influenced by persons of color or other groups subject to oppression and discrimination. Practitioners cannot afford to offend or invalidate the very groups they intend to help and support. Rather, practitioners need to involve these groups in the projects in meaningful ways that provide hope and a sense of enpowerment. Oppressed groups are not children needing nothing more than a "pat on the head." They must not be treated with condescension. They must be involved as equal, competent, thinking actors who have much to contribute to the process—otherwise, all is for naught.

Many citizens do not see life as fair, nor do they really believe they have any power or control over their immediate environment, let alone the larger community. Being involved in a meaningful project can energize people enormously. It is typically a compliment to people to be invited to participate in a project that improves the quality of life for them, their family, and their neighborhood. Sound organization, a common cause, and the ability to act can both promote and reflect empowerment.

The secret to working with groups around volatile issues is to keep them from "locking up" over minutiae and emotional undertones. Practitioners must keep the focus on the big issue—the problem to be addressed—and through deductive reasoning move slowly to specifics. If practitioners let groups get into fine details or definitions too early, little movement is likely. When discussion does turn to details, about which disagreement is more likely, one technique is to let compromise or consensus work for a time and to then call for a "straw vote." This nonbinding vote reveals how close the group is to agreement. Then the practitioner can help the group to address the remaining concerns and move on. The basic idea is for practitioners to keep the focus on areas of agreement and mutuality and work from there.

Kirst-Ashman and Hull (1997B) offer a nice model that summarizes the decision making skills discussed in this chapter. Readers, as they review the processes listed, should begin to see how to select a particular model of change for a particular situation. Readers can use this framework as a way to integrate the detailed information presented in this and previous chapters:

P: Identify **p**roblems to address.

R: **R**eview your macroreality.

E: **E**stablish primary goals.

P: Identify **p**eople of influence.

A: **A**ssess potential financial costs and benefits to clients and agency.

R: Evaluate professional and personal **r**isk.

E: **E**valuate the potential success of a macrochange process.

Problem identification is obviously central to all practice. Next Kirst-Ashman and Hull raise an issue that we have talked about in a variety of ways: What does the practitioner know about *community realities?* Does the practitioner start with a supportive environment in which to work? Does the practitioner have the resources needed to be successful? Can the practitioner access those resources? Has the practitioner identified opposition? Can the opposition's fears be overcome, and if so how? Is the system open to change? Force field analysis (presented in chap. 2) is one analytical tool that can be helpful in determining whether a project is doable, and in *establishing goals* more generally. Next the practitioner must *identify power brokers,* indigenous leaders, and others who can contribute to achieving those goals.

Assessing costs and benefits to the clients and the agency is an important step that is sometimes overlooked. There are costs in any project, even the good ones. For example, there will be financial costs associated with a volunteer-staffed crisis or hotline. Telephone, space, and training are but a few of the specific costs. More indirectly, certain projects and proposals may produce adverse public responses that make funders, current and future, less receptive to funding requests. On the other hand, certain change projects and proposals may increase the respect and credibility accorded to the change group. This may have subsequent financial benefits for the change group.

Projects can also have costs that are not financial. Community backlash against a project can be worse than the ills the project is meant to remedy. For example, *risk to the practitioner's* personal credibility and influence in a small, conservative community may be too great a price for winning the right to distribute birth control devices to junior high school girls. There may be better ways of dealing with teenage pregnancies. This practice warning applies particularly to taking on a major power broker. Even if the practitioner's group wins the initial encounter with an opposing influential, that person may be in a position to make the group pay for that victory at a later date. People have long memories. Practitioners should always *evaluate strategies* based on their likelihood of long-term success.

Practitioners must be careful not to exhaust their resources to win single battles; they must look to the war—and the peace. *Always* leave a way for an opponent to save face. Remember, practitioners should conduct themselves rationally and reasonably; they should not personalize differences or conflict, setting people up to be emotionally damaged or destroyed.

Reasonable people will differ with a practitioner over even critical issues. This doesn't make them the practitioner's enemies. Stay away from namecalling and mudslinging. The same people or groups who oppose the practitioner on one issue may be the strongest allies on another day—that is, if the practitioner has not alienated them.

Integrity and the respect of others is what makes a person influential. An unscrupulous course of action may keep a practitioner from ever being influential or successful in the community again. No community is big enough for a practitioner to remain unscathed by a failure to maintain integrity. It may be years before the practitioner's past resurfaces, but people remember, and they will greet any new proposals with skepticism at the least, and more likely with hostility. Conversely, a practitioner with a consistent record of integrity and skill becomes more and more sought after. People want to know that a practitioner can be trusted, that the practitioner will always place integrity above expediency. Then, and only then, will they risk making a commitment.

A primary principle of conflict resolution is to keep the focus of change on issues and away from anything that even suggests personality attacks. While we may differ with the view of others, we must never stoop to namecalling or mudslinging. Always treat others with respect, and do not impugn their personal integrity. It's one thing to be a formidable foe, but it is another to be an assassin. Do the right things for the right reasons.

CONCLUSION

In this chapter we discussed change, and methodological approaches to change. We introduced the use of key informants and the complexities of board dynamics and composition. We also explored the realities of conflict and decision-making processes. Issues related to integrity and the appropriateness of group composition underpinned the entire chapter.

CHAPTER 7

Exercising Leadership

Practitioners who work in organizations and communities invariably need to provide leadership and to work effectively in public forums. These practitioners must realize that leadership can be exercised through the purposeful use of self both in direct ways and in collaboration with others in indirect ways.

In chapter 3 we talked about the structure of organizations in terms of roles, their relations to each other, and the purposeful orchestration of resources into programs in line with their missions. To some degree that earlier discussion was incomplete because it laid little stress on the leadership role of boards and of people who perform key administrative function in organizations. Similarly, there is the potential for leadership to emanate from bodies outside the organization. Much of practice involves assessing how leadership should be exercised given the goals being pursued and how practitioners should directly or indirectly use themselves to address practice concerns.

Two approaches to the practitioner's role as leader need to be considered. While both approaches speak to role and behavior, they are as much philosophical as methodological; indeed, any social worker's approach to leadership will be heavily influenced by the worker's values, beliefs, and moral reasoning. We now present *servant leadership* and *collaborative leadership*.

So much in the leadership literature focuses on the central theme of power. Basically practitioners are taught the importance of understanding and identifying power, its use, and its distribution within institutions, organizations, and communities. The traditional conceptualization of power is antithetical to servant and collaborative leadership. In these approaches leadership is not something sought or built upon. In fact, if it occurs at all, it is an artifact or by-product of the change process.

To be a servant-leader is to be a servant first. In essence, serving others comes first and underlies and motivates the practitioner's behavior. As a servant the practitioner, whether leading or following, is always searching, listening, and offering hope. By serving, providing a validating example, and refraining from being an authority with all the answers, the practitioner eventually obtains the trust of those being served. This philosophy does not suggest functioning without goals or direction, however. To the contrary, the practitioner must keep the agreed upon goal and dream before the group at all times (Greenfield, 1995). The secret is the practitioner's ability to serve in a manner that empowers the group.

This approach may sound impractical and useless, but there are ethnic and minority populations who simply will not accept outside influence until the professional demonstrates clearly that he or she is trustworthy and genuinely concerned about the people and not furthering a personal or agency agenda. Many populations resist anyone who is not familiar with their culture and who cannot or will not speak their language. To communicate with Mexican migrant farmworkers or garment workers in New York City in Spanish is to respect them and validate them as people of worth. The key to success is found in listening and understanding. Influence can take place only as the practitioner accepts and understands. There is no way that a practitioner can help disenfranchised groups without demonstrating genuine caring, trust and respect. Good intentions are not enough.

Collaborative leadership is a process wherein willing participants interact in a way that blurs roles, as individual members talk with one another, develop common experiences and understanding, and create a shared language that provides for enough meaning to allow consensus (Clift et al., 1995). This process rejects any suggestion that only others will change; it requires that every participant be prepared and willing to change. Collaborative leadership is very difficult for people who need to control situations or who wish to assert the power they enjoy due to position. Many agency directors, public officials, and business owners can become anxious at the ambiguity of interacting, conducting meetings, and participating in problem-solving activities in a democratic, horizontal fashion. The prospect of "coming to the table" simply as an equal may be unique and stressful experience for them. Many social workers also struggle with these fears as they are required to "check at the door" their credentials, degrees, and the supposed authority or expertise associated with their professional, social, and community roles. Moreover, collaborative leadership can be very slow and tedious, as participants work out their individual needs and their assumptions about how the world should be. Even people who come to the table with what appears to be little power may have misgivings about entering into deliberations and problem-solving activities as equals. These people may believe that they in fact gain power by positioning themselves as victims or oppressed groups. So to invite them to give up what little leverage they feel they enjoy by asking them to act as equals can be quite disconcerting; they may be convinced they are giving up their only card.

These two approaches, servant leadership and collaborative leadership, are clearly in direct opposition to a traditional approach that we might call *Machiavellian leadership*. Machiavelli was a fifteenth–sixteenth-century Italian statesman, and his notion of leadership was most striking. Machiavellian leadership is predicated on the assumptions that people are basically fallible, gullible, untrustworthy, and weak; that they should be treated as impersonal objects; and that they are to be manipulated so the leader might achieve his or her goals. This approach is underpinned by utilitarian calculation rather than moral reasoning. Many politicians and institutional directors hold this philosophy. They begin with the assumption that their constituencies are so uninformed that they can't possibly understand the issues. These leaders therefore feel no compunction about thinking for others—of course, always to the benefit of the "benevolent dictator" or the organization with which he or she is involved (Johnson & Johnson, 1994). Unfortunately, some people still embrace such utilitarian thinking. They presume make our choices for us and are quick to put into place programs and policies that can have profound effects on the "voiceless" in society.

CLARIFYING LEADERSHIP: ACTORS AND FUNCTIONS

"Leadership" is one of those terms that everyone uses in roughly the same way, but without fully clarifying many specifics. It is therefore useful to delineate a few specific points that affect practice. We will attempt to blend the ideas of servant leadership and collaborative leadership with more traditional information about this powerful practice dynamic.

First, leadership can be characterized by a set of rationally integrated steps: It defines a person or people who strongly influence, even define, where an organization or community wishes to go. It also denotes a major role in shaping how actually to move toward the realization of some vision. Finally, it suggests the provision of an atmosphere in which appropriate process can operate to help ensure that vision's attainment.

Second, leadership can be seen as a property of person. A person may have "natural" leadership abilities: she or he may have clear ideas about where movement should be directed, be effective in taking instrumental steps to get to the desired state, and have the ability to produce a good, collaborative working style. But leadership can also be characterized by roles and functions. Some assert that leadership is all about influence and that influence inheres in the roles individual group members play at specific times during meetings. Simply put, a person is a leader whenever his or her ideas and actions influence the thoughts and behavior of the group.

In more structural terms, however, certain roles must routinely participate in leadership activities. Among them are board members, top administrators of agencies, and key community actors. Ideally, "natural" leaders would occupy these roles in order to produce vision, strategy, and process. Realistically, however, few practitioners are born leaders (Johnson & Johnson, 1994); therefore each of these three roles presents unique challenges to practitioners in terms of their use of self—whether direct or indirect. (Interestingly, these roles, which *require* leadership, are often thought to *confer* leadership. What these roles in fact confer is legitimate authority. As indicated in chap. 4, this authority may or may not translate into power. What's being suggested is that power and authority are often associated with the concept of leadership and the positions occupied by leaders—but these are four different concepts.)

The three roles—boards, top administrators, and key community actors— have distinct and specific functions. These are discussed below.

Boards

The term, "board" denotes a body of people that oversees and is responsible for the organization itself. In examining boards of different organizations, one overall function is always apparent: it is the board that is responsible for creating policy for the organization. Further, it is the board that attempts periodically to state the general purpose of the organization—in other words, the board articulates mission and vision. Stating that boards are primarily mission- and policy-making bodies in no way implies that boards should engage in either set of activities in a closed fashion; effective boards are becoming more open to the perceptions of key staff, administrators, consultants, forces in the community, outside funders, and so on. Finally, the board has general oversight responsibilities for its organization, especially in use of fiscal resources.

Since boards are collective by nature, there is an increasing trend for boards to be diverse in some range of qualities or characteristics (gender, race, types of professional training and work experiences, age, social connections, and so on). By virtue of its diversity the board is able to reflect and promote a more appropriate range of behaviors in the organization.

A board always has a president (usually elected by the board members) and an executive director who works with it. Much of the time an uneasy tension exists between the board and these leaders. While executive directors and board presidents do not enjoy being micromanaged, they must constantly guard against any inclination to assume more authority than granted by their boards. In general, they work at the pleasure of the board.

The relation between boards and leaders is dynamic and full of energy. The secret to success is keeping all parties working together and not having the group or the leadership going off on its own. It is also important that individual board members not act independently and without the knowledge or approval of the board. Major problems can occur when individual board members presume to speak or act for the board. Ultimately, the activity of any board member can become the concern of the entire board. It is sometimes difficult for enthusiastic individuals to think in terms of the "we-ness" of a collectively.

Top Administrators

Because boards exist through time and determine mission and policy statements, as well as provide general oversight of the organization, their activities must be connected somehow to the structured use of organizational resources. This is the role of the administrator of the organization. In addition, the administrator has the major responsibility to ensure the performance of functions and processes necessary for the organization to exist and to change over time. These include planning, staffing, directing, controlling, and evaluating functions:

Planning has to do with setting goals, specifying means, and setting time expectations.

Organizing has to do with structuring roles to each other so that specific tasks are done to achieve goals.

Staffing has to do with determining and meeting human resource needs, training and developing staff, and linking people's performance to organizational goals.

Directing has to do with the interpersonal activities needed to guide, motivate, instruct, and supervise people to meet organizational goals.

Evaluating has to do with measuring standards and working with the outcomes of such measurements.

Controlling has to do with checking that activities of people in roles accord with set standards, as well as setting specific standards.

All of these activities are carried out by the administrator, who ideally conveys the cumulative organizational experience to the board, which then can carry out its general oversight and mission- and policy-related activities. Top administrators invariably have responsibility for all these tasks but seldom if ever full authority to carry them out in isolation and without board approval. They are truly facilitators who see that the board's will is carried out. While they are significant and while they can literally make or break an organization, top administrators are nonetheless subject to the board and not private entrepreneurs.

Key Community Actors

These are people who over time are seen as being able to articulate the concerns, feelings, and interests of some group or coalition of groups in the community. Typically, these actors have a history of investing their time and, possibly, skills in pursuit of general goals (e.g., the "community good") or specific concerns (e.g., more police protection in a given part of town). Besides their ongoing investment of time and enthusiasm, these people are over time afforded a certain amount of sanction from both community members and perhaps the organizational leaders who are the object of community concern and activity.

Their history of motivated behavior and their high credibility in the community make these actors critical in establishing effective communication between the community and an organization. In fact, some organizations purposefully invite such key actors onto their boards or onto ad hoc committees.

Against the backdrop of all these actors engaging in leadership, there is also the practitioner. As we will see later in the chapter, some practitioners can attempt to be leaders on their own; others will try to work though the leadership actors discussed above.

PROMOTING BOARD ENDS

Practitioners who work with boards, or with selected board members, must reflect in their practice awareness of the products that are the domain of boards: policy, mission, and general oversight, which includes fiduciary responsibility. This broad purview can be translated into specific guidelines for the practitioner.

First, the practitioner must be able to make necessary information available to the board. This can sometimes be done via direct communication; but typically, it is done through a key administrator in the organization. The practitioner attempts to provide the following types of information about both the ends and the means of the organization:

1. Who are the clients coming to the organization and who are not?
2. Which clients is the organization serving on a continuing basis and which are being sent elsewhere?
     (Both items 1 and 2 require purposeful and systematic collection of data, discussed in chap. 3.)
3. What are the current, pressing needs and risks in the community?
4. What are the responses of other programs and services?
5. What trends (patterns over time) are emerging in populations, problems, and responses?
6. What needs specific to the organization's mission are being addressed?
7. What has been the outcome of interventions by the organization?
8. What is the continuing justification for existing service strategies?
9. What is the current reality of available resources for existing strategies?
10. What new or potential resources should be considered or pursued?
11. What is the degree of fit between values and purposes in the mission statement and ongoing organizational experiences, viewed from a systems perspective?

Obviously, the last item involves putting together information about most of the other concerns and then viewing it against the backdrop of values and philosophy. Many agencies and boards have a difficult time restricting their activities to those identified in their mission statements. If not cautioned against violating their mandates, agencies and boards may want to expand their services beyond what they are authorized to do. This phenomenon is often described as "being all things to all people."

Now, in itemizing some specific topics that boards should consider as they engage in policy, mission, and oversight functions we cannot assume they know either the "right" questions or whom to ask. It is precisely in this context that practitioners perceive the importance of process and atmosphere.

To promote appropriate board behavior and inquiry and to prevent unpredictable and even inappropriate communication between boards and practitioners, it is necessary to identify what practitioners can bring to board deliberations so as to maximize appropriate board behavior. This subject will be developed later in the chapter.

Practitioners must project an air of availability and willingness to provide information—though perhaps indirectly, through key administrators. Specifically, practitioners attempt to convey that they have access to data. Their attitude must communicate questions of the following kind: Which pieces of the process do you—the board—want to be responsible for? Do you wish me or other organizational staff to work with committees of the board? Appropriate delegation and assignment of specific responsibility, essential to successful board activity, must be elicited.

Practitioners must realize, however, that this indirect strategy of availability and willingness to provide data does not always produce the desired effect. When this is the case practitioners, again through key administrators who have direct board contact, may have to ask some of the above questions explicitly and then present relevant information to the appropriate parties— for example, a planning committee of the board.

About this more explicit approach several cautions need to be raised: Don't assume at first that board members want information—in fact, they may not want any major initiatives from agency staff. The reason may lie in the agency's history or in board concerns that new strategies of communication (parties and content) indicate staff power plays. Boards often suspect the motives of professional staff and practitioners and will almost automatically resist recommendations from the staff. This initial resistance can, however, be quite productive as board members become engaged in the process and as the practitioner "sharpens" the original proposal and the rationale for the recommendation.

To minimize possible board resistance to relevant information, the practitioner's tone of communication should stress clear recognition of the board's exclusive role in policy-related matters. Similarly, if data can be presented in a format that suggests that it is the board's responsibility to come up with an appropriate response, the communication from the practitioner has a better chance of being heard and considered. It is wise to remind board members periodically that they make the decisions and thus have the last word. The practitioner's job is simply to see that they have the information and data needed for reasoned decisions and then to successfully implement those decisions. Boards do funny things at times, and they will mix roles and responsibilities in such a way as to have the practitioner assume more responsibility than she or he should. Although this may seem to be to the practitioner's benefit on a particular occasion, the abdication of responsibility by the board may ultimately backfire, with the practitioner left "holding the bag." Practitioners should watch carefully and keep lines of authority and responsibility clear.

Specific to this last mentioned point, practitioners, as they assist in the board leadership process, will sometimes have to lay out the relative positives and negatives (costs and benefits) associated with the data. In this way the practitioner begins to assist the board in defining and selecting important decision criteria. Clearly, the practitioner minimizes the negatives that could be associated with the itemized costs and benefits by specifying some as "possible examples" and indicating that the board will have to determine the actual decision criteria.

During this process of focused communication the board passes through four stages of deliberation:

1. Collecting a body of information on the items under consideration—for example, monthly statistical reports that are really snapshots of the organization relative to population, problems, and responses

2. Comparing the reporting period's snapshot, or profile, to a comparable profile in the past—for example, last month, last quarter, or last year

3. Looking at the profiles in stages 1 and 2 in relation to the system's environment in terms of funding, population need and risk, and service changes

4. Considering possible changes (policy or mission) in the organization

As the practitioner helps the board to move from developing actual responses to examining continued adherence to existing policy and mission, directly or indirectly the practitioner is encouraging the board to revisit the values, purposes, and philosophy of the organization. These identity-related activities are normal; all organizations do something like them, though with varying frequency. Here we are suggesting that the practitioner lead, usually indirectly, by promoting communication and the board's systematic use of certain information. Remember that when the board makes decisions that fall outside current policy, the members must be made aware of what they are doing. Current decisions must be predicated on reliable data and information and not made by default because the board did not really understand what it was doing or being asked to do.

One final thought involves the reality of interests. Organizations, and their board members, don't routinely act altruistically. They have interests precisely because they are *organizations:* they collectively represent a unique distillation of actors, values, and experiences. When an organization engages in behavior that is not prescribed by its current position (which embodies its past), there is a strong possibility it will attempt to meet its interests. In some cases the interests being served are tied to noble values; in other cases they are not.

When practitioners understand the imperatives and interests of organizations—continued existence, name, prestige, influence, and so on—they can facilitate the leadership process by linking organizational interests to professional concerns and real community needs. For example, the after-school needs of single parents might "require" an organization to develop a program in response. This program would meet real needs and would be consistent with the identified mission of the organization. In addition, it has the potential to be a powerful fund-raising tool or could be used to compensate for a previous service fiasco.

PROMOTING BOARD PROCESS

The preceding discussion, which focused on communication and information relative to the ends and means that boards pursue, already introduced the issues of process and atmosphere. The aim of leadership is not just a cognitively derived product (policy and mission, in the case of a board) that implies a set of logical, utilitarian responses and strategies. Also central to effective leadership is the atmosphere and affective component of group activity. Board members are real people with feelings and emotions, and they need to feel some satisfaction and fulfillment of they may not remain on the board or be as productive as they can be. Such fulfillment can, and should, come from performing the functions needed to accomplish group tasks. All board members must realize that in the end, they are the ones who suggest ideas, frame problems, offer solutions, and so on. Each and every one of them is potentially important and has something to offer the organization.

Board members must be encouraged to seek additional information, especially in the eleven areas listed in the preceding section. They should also be encouraged to seek each other's opinions on the meaning of the information received and to think about the commonalities and differences in the opinions and data presented. Beyond this, board members must be encouraged to share information that emanates from their own unique experiences. Members need to feel that their opinions are worth offering and worth hearing for others. In sum, the active exchange of both "hard" data and opinion must be the substance of board process.

The interactive flow of information and opinion must be accompanied by the elaboration and development of thoughts and key points. Board members should attempt to look for linking thoughts and expressions. As this communication process builds, key points should be summarized and, when possible, agreed upon. Eventually all the information is collected, sifted, clarified, analyzed, and organized into a proposal.

RECOGNIZING BOARD ROLES

Board members play various roles during their meetings. Practitioners should learn to recognize the roles as they appear in the board process and, moreover, to play necessary roles that are missing themselves until board members feel comfortable enough to assume them.

Beal, Bohlen, and Raudabaugh (1967) have created a thoughtful classification of the roles that group members play as they interact with one another. They suggest three broad classes of roles: group task roles, group building and maintenance roles, and individual roles.

Group task roles are exactly what the name implies. In essence, individuals playing these roles focus on the task at hand, and their roles facilitate and coordinate group activity so that the task can be successfully completed. Practitioners should not assume that people who play these roles do so consciously. They are often just being themselves and doing what comes naturally. Let's double back for a moment and make another connection. Task roles are primarily cognitive roles and are taken by individuals who often "act" from their heads and not necessarily from their hearts. They are programmed (by nature and upbringing) to be thinkers, doers, and problem solvers. It drives them absolutely crazy to be in groups that are not committed and oriented to action. They want to move on and get things done now. They tend to have little empathy for people who need to be stroked, coddled, and loved. It's not that they don't care about others or that they don't have feelings, but they are clearly motivated by the need to accomplish things.

The group roles and behaviors performed by **task**-oriented individuals include:

Role	Behaviors
Initiator-contributor	Proposes new ideas; offers suggestions for change
Information seeker	Asks for clarification; seeks factual and authoritative data
Opinion seeker	Seeks clarification of values rather than facts; desires ideas from others
Information giver	Offers facts; is authoritative
Opinion giver	States beliefs of opinions not based on relevant facts or information
Elaborator	Spells out suggestions with examples; develops meanings; offers rationales for suggestions previously made
Summarizer	Pulls ideas, suggestions, and comments together so group knows where they are
Coordinator-integrator	Clarifies relations between various ideas and suggestions; takes ideas from each member and integrates into meaningful whole

Orienter	Defines position of group with respect to its goals
Disagreer	Takes different point of view; argues against; spots errors in logic; acts as devil's advocate
Evaluator-critic	Subjects accomplishments to set of standards
Energizer	Prods group to action; stimulates group
Procedural technician	Expedites group activity; performs routine tasks
Recorder	Writes down suggestions and group decisions; serves as group memory (Beal, Bohlen, & Raudabaugh, 1967)

These constructs won't be developed further, but the list gives an overview of the activities performed by task-oriented board members. They keep the board working, focused, and outcome oriented. While all of the roles identified are positive and needed, if played to the extreme and not balanced by building and maintenance roles, they can become problematic and dysfunctional. The board can become very frustrated with members who don't know when to back down from roles they are playing. For example, the information seeker wants factual information on which to base a reasoned decision. When this role is pursued too aggressively, however, other board members can become unsettled as they are constantly quizzed for "chapter and verse." or substantiation for everything being discussed.

The second class of roles are *group building and maintenance roles*. People who fulfill these roles are deeply concerned about the way the group is functioning and the way its members are feeling. They focus on the affective, emotional, interpersonal aspects of the group and see as their primary role strengthening, regulating, and perpetuating the group *as a group*. Again, their actions are often not consciously motivated, rather they are a product of the natural self. It isn't that these people aren't interested in the group's task of the board; it's more that they are interested in bringing the whole group along and making sure that members feel good about the process and their individual contributions.

The group roles and behaviors performed by building-and-maintenance–oriented individuals include:

Role	*Behaviors*
Encourager	Praises; agrees with and accepts contributions; is warm and praising
Harmonizer	Mediates; attempts to reconcile disagreements
Compromiser	Seeks compromise; yields status; admits error; comes halfway
Gatekeeper and expediter	Encourages participation of others; proposes regulation of flow of communication

Standard setter or ego ideal	Expresses group standards; evaluates quality of group processes
Group observer and commentator	Keeps records; feeds data back to group with proposed interpretations
Follower	Goes along with group; is passive; accepts ideas of others; serves as an audience (Beal, Bohlen, & Raudabaugh, 1967)

All of the specific roles identified under the general heading of group building and maintenance are positive. However, like the task roles, they can be dysfunctional when played to excess. For example, the harmonizer and the compromiser can work so hard at "pouring oil on troubled waters" that they won't permit conflict and the energy that flows from this powerful dynamic. Productive group activity is predicated on a diversity of ideas. Conflict, differentness, and tension should not be avoided; rather they should be encouraged. These dynamics can indeed make some board members uncomfortable—until they realize that the conflict is between different ideas, not different personalities.

The third class of roles are *individual roles,* and they are generally more negative than positive. No attempt should be made to suppress these roles because they can produce important information; however, these roles can become quite problematic for the group leader. People playing these roles are satisfying their own needs. The roles are irrelevant to the group task and are, typically, counterproductive to building and maintenance.

Individual roles and behaviors include:

Role	*Behaviors*
Aggressor	Deflates others; attacks, envies, and disapproves of others
Blocker	Is negative and stubborn; opposes and disagrees beyond reason
Recognition seeker	Calls attention to self; boasts
Self-confessor	Expresses personal, non-group-oriented feelings, insights, and ideologies
Playboy	Lacks involvement; is nonchalant and cynical; indulges in horseplay
Dominator	Manipulates; asserts authority or superiority
Help seeker	Calls for sympathy; is insecure and self-deprecating
Special interest pleader	Is dishonest by cloaking own biases and prejudices by pretending to speak on behalf of others (Beal, Bohlen, & Randabaugh, 1967)

Knowing the exact names of the roles identified above isn't important; understanding the behavior associated with each role is. Especially important is the distinction between task behaviors and building and maintenance behaviors. Practitioners working with boards or community groups will be challenged when task people push for authoritative information, facts, and action and building and maintenance people assert that the task at hand is taking precedence over people. Task people can be crisp or unresponsive to comments they consider shallow, nonsubstantive, or non-goal-oriented. They will hold to the agenda and become agitated when others want to divert from the task at hand. Sometimes they are less relaxed and less personal than other board members would like. The bottom line, nevertheless, is that boards need all kinds of people, and practitioners need to be able to recognize when key roles aren't being played.

When key roles are obviously missing from a group, it is necessary for the group leader to step up and assume them. For example, a neighborhood group might be so homogeneous and laid back that no one is inclined to play any of the task roles. If the leader is unable to get some task roles going, nothing constructive will occur. The group members may enjoy being together, but time will show that nothing substantive ever really happens.

Many practitioners recognize that they identify far more with one of the two major classes of positive roles than with the other. For example, they may be aware that they have no difficulty staying on task, while others appear to be more concerned about interpersonal relationships and having a warm supportive environment than about pursuing the meeting's agenda. This is normal and should *not* be a concern. Remember, the key to success as a group leader is personal awareness. It is possible, with self-discipline, to learn to play different roles and contribute different behaviors. Because many leaders have personal worries about group process, however, at the end of the next section we briefly discuss dealing with ambivalence.

BEING A LEADER

Having raised the concept of leadership it is useful to move into a practical discussion of how practitioners can produce a positive atmosphere that maintains and promotes group process. Practitioners through their use of self attempt to:

1. *Encourage*—The practitioner encourages, primarily by example, a climate of friendliness, warmth, and responsiveness, that promotes contributions from everyone and is characterized by positive reinforcement.

2. *Promote full participation*—The practitioner focuses on the appropriate balance of communication from all participants, largely by acting as chair of the meeting. In all meetings there is a risk that some group members

will dominate the communication process. When this happens the group doesn't own the topic, and the group-building process is endangered. Conversely, some members can be reticent about offering ideas and thoughts to the group. In both instances the chair must respond—for example: "We've heard a lot of good ideas from Mary and Bob. Does anyone have additional ideas?" "Are there other ways to look at this in addition to the way Bob is suggesting?" Some quiet group members may even need specific encouragement: "We have heard from many concerning their thoughts. How about you, Mary—what do you think?" Sometimes a general statement can address both situations at once: "Let's try to limit the time for remarks so that everyone has a chance to offer thoughts and ideas."

3. *Adhere to norms*—All groups must arrive at working standards about what constitutes appropriate subject matter, how business will proceed, and how the group will periodically examine its own functioning. Central to all three areas is the notion of an agenda. Agendas require that the content of each meeting be planned ahead of time. Typically, the agenda is set by a small group: the chair may work with just one key staff member, such as the practitioner. The set of agendas ideally ties meetings together, and each agenda structures the process in the actual meeting. An agenda gives the chair and the board members a framework within which to operate and helps to define the appropriate range of discussion.

Group members need to learn that only items on the formal agenda will be discussed. Occasionally, the group will opt to modify the agenda at the beginning of the meeting. This should be the exception, however; or before long the agenda is worthless.

Actual meetings rarely cover all topics fully, and therefore agendas, over time, contain "old" business as well as "new" business. The agenda setters need to be cautious, however, that old business is not forever carried over from the end of one agenda to the end of the next. Either an item comes to the table or it should be omitted from the next agenda though some judgment should be used in removing undiscussed items.

Agendas can also document other activities. Items presented for resolution or vote can be specified, for example. Similarly, the formation of working groups or subgroups can be recorded, as can the results of their deliberations when they are reported to the entire group. Thus old business, new business, and reports from working groups constitute the structure of most meetings. With this kind of structure and flow in place the group can always pause and look at its own record and can introduce modifications, new directions, even new working groups.

4. *Encourage active listening and expression of group feelings*—Active listening starts with not interrupting others, and includes "allowing" others to offer opinions and information. Beyond this it means listening in a way that is

both cognitive and affective. By listening cognitively a person is thinking: Do I understand? Do I agree? By listening affectively (to the nonverbal) a person is asking: Does this feel right? Does the rest of the group intuit what is being said as theirs? Can I embrace this as my own? This process can be heightened in group members if the leader summarizes the issue being discussed and the feelings being conveyed by the person speaking. In this way the group can react to and reinforce both the cognitive and affective components of the communication. When this occurs the group really bonds and ownership of what is being expressed becomes truly collective.

5. *Mediate and reduce tension*—Not all communication within groups leads to full positive expression or total group ownership. The leader must attempt to set up a process that allows compromises to be found and differences between members to be settled constructively. This is not a separate stage; it is done through all the other elements discussed. Group members must learn that reasonable people can differ, that reasonable people can explore together particular areas of agreement while being in some state of disagreement, and that the unifying norm of respect can help people to "agree to disagree"—that is, disagreeing in an agreeable way. When disagreements do occur in an agreeable way, the group leader brings the participants back to what has been agreed on and what should flow from the areas of agreement. In short, what is the common ground—what is owned by the group? The leader can refocus discussion on what members actually agree about by citing the group's history or prior experience: "Last year when we got into this type of situation, remember we decided to . . ." or "Last year we agreed that we could all commit ourselves to . . ."

6. *Observe, assess, and evaluate*—As the leader and group work together, a group process, or flow, emerges, and it becomes clear that some tasks are getting done. However, the process is not always functional, nor is it certain that the "right" tasks are being done in a timely manner. Failure on either front threatens the group itself. Therefore, the group leader is always watching for difficulties within the group in terms of how members communicate and work with each other. Possible issues are dysfunctional communication patterns, mistiming of discussion items and participant comments, inadequate and ill-timed work outside group meetings, inappropriate agenda setting, and perceived autocratic leadership. For example, board members will really struggle if they find their leader too autocratic or authoritarian. Most board members are very capable people and as such are likely to resent being controlled of parented. Depending on the area of concern the group can take new steps that can subsequently be evaluated.

The way a practitioner approaches and conducts the business identified in these six overlapping tasks is critical to the ultimate success of the project in question. While leadership style isn't the practitioner's only consideration in professional activity, it is nonetheless a significant factor in professional success or failure. Three leadership styles have been identified over time: authoritarian (autocratic), democratic (egalitarian), and laissez-faire (hands off). Many social workers identify with a particular style and regard the other styles as inappropriate. A note of caution about such thinking: practitioners must learn to be comfortable using all three styles. It is imperative that the leadership role accommodate the needs of the group and not the preference of the practitioner. For the most part, practitioners use democratic and laissez-faire styles; however, some groups at some times require a more direct, more authoritarian approach. This may simply mean that in the early stages of a group's work, its members are so inexperienced and unfamiliar with the process and expectations of the leader that they need more direction to get started. In some respects this approach is more "authoritative" than authoritarian, but it may seem very directive and thus in the minds of some members quite controlling.

While most practitioners are familiar with the concept of leadership styles, Carlisle offers an interesting variation on the traditional notions (Skidmore, 1995). We present a modified version of Carlisle's user-friendly classification:

	Style		
Condition	Directive (Authoritarian)	Participative (Democratic)	Free-Rein (Laissez-Faire)
Focus	Leader centered	Group centered	Individual centered
Decisions	Leader makes most decisions	Subordinates involved in decisions	Subordinates make decisions
Independence	Little freedom of action	Some independence	Almost complete independence
Communication	One way	Two way	Free, open
Power	Leader uses power and discipline	Leader tries to persuade, not force	Leader relies on self-control
Subordinates' feelings	Little concern for subordinates' feelings	Subordinates' feelings considered	Subordinates' feelings predominate
Orientation	Task centered	People and group centered	Individual accomplishment centered
Leader's role	Provide direction	Involve group	Provide support resources
Psychological	Obedience and dependency	Cooperation and participation	Independence and individual performance

Before bringing this chapter to a close, we raise two important points. The first point concerns the whole notion of *who leads the group*. We have spent considerable time clarifying the dynamics that practitioners must consider as they take on the "assumed role" of community organizer, administrator, chair of committee or board, and so forth; however, other considerations need to be explored. There is a body of literature placing the heart of leadership in the ability to influence others and work through and with others. Leadership is not the property solely of the identified or self-appointed leader. Indeed, as discussed in the first section of this chapter, some people assert that leadership is not an individual property at all but rather is characterized by functions and roles. Simply put, any member of a group can take action that serves the group function and thus lead or influence the group. Leadership functions can be fulfilled by different members, at different times, performing activities and roles that contribute to the success of the group (Johnson & Johnson, 1995). This observation clearly suggests that influence is specific to a situation. Despite the skeptics who think this notion is too simplistic, it is reason for practitioners to seriously consider the value of those with whom they work and those whom they serve—and not to take themselves too seriously.

The second point focuses on the *personal conflicts*, or *ambivalence*, practitioners might feel as they take on larger systems. Many practitioners are intimidated by group activity in the first place, and this feeling only intensifies when they try to help make something happen on a larger scale. Too often new practitioners measure themselves against seasoned veterans. To compare is to lose and to become discouraged. Some people seem, by nature, to be more poised and comfortable working with boards and committees, but new practitioners can *learn* to be effective in the macroarena. The secret is self-discipline and the conscious use of self. The greatest challenge is overcoming fear of risking and taking on new roles and activities.

Zaleznik offers suggestions for dealing realistically with inner conflicts and fears:

1. Acknowledge and accept the diversity of group member motivation. Leaders realize that people possess a variety of negative as well as positive feelings.

2. Establish a firm sense of identity. Leaders must understand themselves (strengths and weaknesses).

3. Maintain constancy and continuity in response. Leaders should be consistent in how they present themselves to others.

4. Be very selective in activities and relations. Leaders must understand how to select activities, set priorities, and be able to say no to less important activities.

5. Learn how to communicate. Leaders must be aware of their own reactions and must make their opinions and attitudes known without wasteful delay.

6. Live within a cyclical life pattern. Leaders create a rhythm that allows for various activities during the day. (Skidmore, 1995)

CONCLUSION

In this chapter we developed the key element of leadership in terms of organizational structure and key actors. Atmosphere, role relationships, and group process are critical aims of leadership. Within this complex topic the concept of use of self and work with and through others was stressed.

CHAPTER 8

Evaluating Practice

As professionals, practitioners have to assess their own work. More specifically, they have to determine whether their personal activities and the programs with which they are involved are promoting the changes desired. In this chapter we briefly discuss the core material that practitioners must know if they are to monitor and possibly modify their practices and interventions over time.

USING EVALUATION

Evaluation of practice is worthwhile for a variety of reasons. First, practitioners, as members of a profession, have an obligation to be self-monitoring (Powers, Meenaghan, & Toomey, 1985). They have an ethical obligation to be constructively critical and rational in their practice. Practitioners must verify that the problems or situations they attempt to address are owned by some definable constituency and important enough to warrant purposeful change efforts (Meenaghan & Kilty, 1993). Evaluation suggests that relevance and sanction from those affected are important professional principles.

Second, practitioners must be able to adapt their individual practices over time as they employ a rational problem-solving model within a systems perspective (Tripodi, 1983). Basically this means that some systematic process has to be brought to the study, assessment, and intervention stages discussed in chapter 2. During the study stage the practitioner asks: Am I collecting the right range of data? Am I involving the right people? The practitioner moves next to the assessment stage and examines the possible meaning of the information gathered. Then the practitioner develops a planned response to the problems identified. Finally, the practitioner looks systematically at the results of the interventions selected in light of the study and assessment stages. In order to conduct this kind of evaluation the practitioner needs a mechanism for determining whether the desired effects were achieved, whether the affected parties are satisfied with the results, whether the intervention activities as planned really occurred, and so on. Depending on the feedback

131

received the program may continue with the same interventions or may be modified—perhaps substantially.

Evaluation allows practitioners to adjust not only intervention within the rational problem-solving model but also study and assessment. When a practitioner recognizes the power of evaluation as a process, it ceases to be a threat and becomes an opportunity. Knowing what to ask and why it is necessary allows the practitioner to shape the stages of the problem-solving model into a coherent whole. Without an evaluation component, the problem-solving model, like any other extended procedure, runs the risk of becoming arbitrary or ritualistic, and therefore not rational. Practitioners may choose study and assessment methods haphazardly, with little thought to their utility in designing interventions. Or they may develop quasi-religious commitments to particular interventions or to the theories on which the interventions are based, whether or not they fit the system being addressed. Evaluation does not allow this. The information it provides guides the active participation of practitioners in creating fluid and adaptive change responses (Meenaghan & Kilty, 1994).

Third, practitioners are human beings, seeking fulfilling practice or work experiences. They want to know that what they are doing is on target, that their work is relevant to some group, organization, or community, and that the interventions they carry out are functional (Powers, Meenaghan, & Toomey, 1985). Moreover, true professionals need to know the results of their efforts. It is only as they evaluate their practice that professionals can grow and mature, becoming wiser and more skilled in their evaluations and interventions.

In addition to addressing the professional norm of self-monitoring keeping, the problem-solving model rational and adaptive, and promoting worker self-satisfaction, there are still other reasons for evaluation. Basically, they have to do with political considerations, economics, and the role of key constituencies (Austin, 1982).

The people who pay the costs of programs want answers to critical questions associated with evaluation: Are the problems being addressed relevant? Are the interventions working? Are the interventions being efficiently employed by all staff? Are the overall efforts paid for, in fact, carried out?

Since the time of Nixon, through the Reagan and Clinton eras, there has been an effort to redefine almost all social problems as the result of individual malfunctioning. As a result, these types of questions have become politically charged. They are often motivated by the wish to downsize public and governmental responsibilities. Within this context, evaluation is sometimes seen as a way to justify cutting back resources and abandoning commitments.

These cutbacks at first appear to be an issue only in the public sector, but they have enormous implications for the private sector as well. In fact, the private sector relies heavily on public contracts and reimbursement. As a result, both public and private agencies are today being asked to do more with less, and they are being asked to demonstrate that what they are doing is both socially responsible and effective.

Thus, while evaluation evolved within the profession as a functional and ethical norm associated with good practice, it can also be used to justify retrenchment and short-sighted economies. Given these radically different, even conflicting, views of evaluation, organizations and their practitioners now have little choice but to engage in a range of activities to satisfy the expectations of external funders and, in most cases, internal boards conditioned to emphasize fiscal restraint. The present political climate requires professional practitioners to be astute and knowledgeable about evaluative research so that negative questions and negative assumptions aren't the only agenda driving the process. An unwary practitioner can play into the hands of the "program axers" and not really present a fair look at the agency's overall functioning and its contribution to the community. To conduct research without fully appreciating the possible interplay among context, selected questions, and use of findings may be both unprofessional and unethical.

Funders and boards expect to see evidence that desired activities have occurred (auditing and monitoring), that the cost of activities is justified (efficiency, which involves volume and duration considerations), and that there are positive results that warrant continued funding. Going well beyond these requirements is the use of evaluation to discriminate among competing programs in a context of declining overall resources. In all these cases, evaluation is a tool used to enforce the ultimate expectation: do more with less.

As influential as they are, funders are not the only external constituency that demands evaluation. Many citizens volunteer considerable time to improve their neighborhoods and communities. While they willingly share their talents and provide invaluable service, they want to know that their efforts are making a difference. They want more than just to feel good, they want results. They will demand to know if the collective efforts of the group are meeting the identified goals. If the group's efforts are not effective, they want to know what isn't working and what changes need to occur to assure success (Meenaghan & Kilty, 1993).

All the forces pushing for evaluation make it, now and forever, a critical aspect of all practice. Professional norms and community norms concerning evaluation, though not necessarily the same, may be quite compatible. The expectations of funders, however, bring other dynamics into the evaluation component of practice.

UNDERSTANDING EVALUATION CONTENT

Evaluation should not be regarded as something that takes place only after intervention has started (Tripodi, 1983). Admittedly, some critical examination of practice does occur after intervention activities have been initiated, and after they have been concluded; however, the selection of what the practitioner wishes to achieve is really the start of evaluation. The clearer the practitioner is about desired results, even before designing the intervention, the easier subsequent evaluation becomes.

Basically, evaluation as a process requires the practitioner to determine whether there is a connection between a particular intervention and a particular consequence or set of consequences (Rossi & Freeman, 1982). Outcome and intervention are so intimately linked that if the practitioner cannot specify intended outcomes from a practice intervention, then not only is appropriate evaluation unlikely, so too is defensible, focused practice. In short, evaluation requires that there be clear, measurable outcomes. Such clarity contributes greatly to the precision and relevance of actual practice interventions.

In connecting practice and evaluation, two key considerations are obvious: specificity and timing. *Specificity* means that the practitioner is looking for specific results: for example, more referrals, more utilization of educational opportunities, or increased social contacts. Specificity also demands that the practitioner use specific operationalizations of desired results: for example, greater social contacts as observed through attendance at meetings, increased number of social interactions, and so on. With specificity—the structuring of observations and selection of indicators—the measurement of practice can begin.

Timing means that the practitioner looks for results within a particular time interval: for example, increased social contacts within six months. This suggests that what is observed at the completion of the named interval is capable of being precisely defined, observed, and even measured. The results at the end of the interval can then be contrasted with the state of affairs before the practice intervention occurred, or with the results of other interventions developed for the same purpose.

This discussion of evaluation is intended to suggest the striking and direct connection, through the rational problem-solving model, between the evaluation process and study, assessment, and intervention. Both practice and evaluation emphasize learning as much as possible about the consequences of specific practice interventions. The structured observations obtained during study and assessment guide the design of intervention and, therefore, of evaluation; those obtained during evaluation guide their redesign, if the desired results are not being achieved.

This feedback loop is essential to problem solving and successful practice. Once the practitioner embraces the idea that evaluation is intrinsic to practice, certain predictable practice/evaluation pitfalls become far less likely.

Clear Goals

The first pitfall is not setting clearly articulated goals for practice (Washington, 1980). This can occur in several ways. For example, it can mean thinking of practice and intervention from the standpoint of inputs, or things to be done, for example:

To offer a value clarification program on alcohol to tenth graders

To be a community resource

To be available to . . .

To contribute to . . .

To promote . . .

It's apparent that goals so stated are difficult if not impossible to measure effectively. This kind of practice thought is deficient because it doesn't structure practice behavior enough and it doesn't specify what is to be achieved. The statements listed above are basically meaningless: all they say, in essence, is that some unspecified program-related behavior will produce something that is either unspecified or has variable meaning to different constituencies.

Goals can also fail to be clear because of vagueness. Vagueness can result from having no time frame or from having too few definable parameters attached to the stated intervention, for example:

To contribute to a deeper understanding . . .

To promote a deeper appreciation by the community of . . .

Specific examples of practice/evaluation thought and wording errors can be found in the following goals set by a mental health agency:

To build on the agency's commitment to the Hispanic community

To work more closely with the Hispanic community in the catchment area

To provide outreach services to the Hispanic community

To have a 10 percent increase in referrals from the Hispanic community over the next six months

While all of the above statements suggest *something* about practice intervention, only the last statement triggers meaningful considerations. It sets an observable and measurable target number, 10 percent, and it specifies a time frame. The method of evaluation is now obvious: the practitioner clocks and compares data at two points in time—now and six months later. Most important, this type of goal statement brings focus to the assessment stage: How are we going to get the 10 percent increase? Given the available resources, agency staff might design three program interventions:

The agency will offer three community-wide forums.

Four staff members will make contact with twenty-five key actors in the Hispanic community.

Seven residents of the community will go door to door within Hispanic areas informing people in their homes about the agency and its services.

The clear goal and explicit time frame will encourage agency practitioners to ask whether a specific program strategy worked (Austin, 1982), and even which of the different program strategies was most effective with the various members of the Hispanic community—for example, the young, the old, single parents. In fact, evaluation questions could be framed in a way that produces data on the age and marital status of those continuing service. In short, clarity about goals can and will lead to clarity about outcomes.

Control Groups

Practitioners and others involved in programs must be careful, however, about inferring that positive change or the achievement of the goal is due entirely to the program intervention—a second pitfall of practice/evaluation. The desired outcome could simply reflect changes over time; for example, the increased experience of the Hispanic population could lead them to use community resources better and more effectively. Or some other change—such as the addition of a charismatic professional in the community, say a local clergy-person or someone at the mental health agency—could be the reason for increased use of services by the Hispanic population, rather than the new program.

These two factors, sometimes called "maturation of subjects" and "outside variables," are important to understand and appreciate. If one or both were present but not considered in the evaluation of the new program, a false positive effect could be attributed to the program. That is, the program would be considered a success when in reality it might not be.

To compensate for either of these factors the practitioner should consider whether controls and multiple measures through time would be useful (Campbell & Stanley, 1966). The use of controls involves the comparison of two or more groups through time. They aren't necessarily matched but rather may differ by chance. Multiple measures are used to get a better feel of the dynamics of change, if any, over time.

In the example of outreach to Hispanics in a particular catchment area, agency practitioners might identify two groups on either side of a major arterial and initially offer the outreach program to one group and not the other. Over the six-month period the practitioners would measure the two groups against the designated goal of a 10 percent increase in referrals.

Even in this case practitioners would like to know what is going on qualitatively in the subcommunity that is getting the outreach program. Does it have forces, events, or people who might affect the program or outcome? If a control or comparison subcommunity is involved, the same question applies to it. Obviously, the more practitioners know about the target area and the comparison area, if there is one, the greater the persuasive power of findings about the program intervention being evaluated.

Another control strategy used in some created programs is purposeful comparison between those who receive an intervention and those on a waiting list, who have not yet received it. This strategy avoids the ethical questions raised by withholding services from clients. If the intervention is found to be effective, then those on the waiting list will eventually receive a service that has already been critically examined, and possibly improved.

Respect for People

In the real world of clients and their needs, the quest for controls and multiple measures over time is sometimes more ideal than feasible. Beside the logistics and costs of locating a second Hispanic subcommunity or of applying evaluation measures to people on a waiting list, there are other issues that practitioners must recognize as they serve those in need. They have to remember as they review the different elements of practice—the needs of real clients, the specific needs to be addressed, and research considerations—that research is at most equal to the other elements. However critical research and evaluation may seem, the needs of people have to be respected—intentional denial of service for purposes of research presents real ethical issues (Meenaghan & Kilty, 1993).

Because resources are usually limited, program decisions about implementation typically mean that professionals serve some prioritized people, groups, or areas and not others. Remember, practitioners cannot be all things to all people. If practitioners spread themselves too thin and water their programs down too much, everyone suffers—such programs may not help anyone. Similarly, practitioners must realize that research and evaluation is sometimes the best way to serve people and their needs.

Ideally, chance is used to set up comparison groups. However, when chance is present, real-life contingencies and emergencies of real people typically make blind assignment difficult, if not unethical. Further, it is conceivable that a member of the comparison group may have to move from the nonservice category due to some acute need or development.

Pilot Programs

Beyond the issues raised above—the ideal of research clarity, the possible role of time and the definition of control groups, and the importance and dignity of people and their needs—still another issue remains to be considered: the possible relation between program design and program research, against the background of social and behavioral science knowledge (Rossi & Freeman, 1982).

The logic of experimental design—which is what we have been discussing—is an attempt to see programs as hypotheses to be validated. It asks, for example, whether the following statement is true: if we hold three community-wide forums, referrals from the Hispanic community will rise 10 percent in six months. Comparisons and multiple measures are often necessary for ensuing inferences and judgments. Such designs also typically assume a rather high level of knowledge about a precisely defined set of variables, however; practice in larger systems has not arrived at this point.

In the real world practitioners often don't even know how many variables are involved, let alone have validated knowledge about them and the relations among them. Put another way, the level of validated knowledge that underpins the design of programs rarely meets the conditions for a valid experiment. Many times practitioners have limited knowledge, limited practice wisdom, and only anecdotal information on which to base evaluative designs. They find themselves without enough information and, at times, expertise to feel confident in moving forward with a program strategy that will remain fixed for six months or a year.

When this is the case, an intervention should be regarded as a *pilot program*. Rather than testing with precision a small number of intervention phenomena, a pilot program is an instrumental way to collect more and better information and possibly to help the pilot groups. As new information is collected, more precise practice statements can be made, and an experimental design can be considered that both fits the purposes of the program and assists in the acquisition of validated data. In sum, far more programs are better seen as candidates for pilot programming than for advanced experimental testing (Meenaghan, Washington, & Ryan, 1982).

DISTINGUISHING EVALUATION FROM ACCOUNTABILITY

Practitioners should not assume that the concepts of evaluation and accountability are interchangeable. In a strict sense, formal evaluation is a measure that makes accountability possible. Yet it is not the only one: power, especially political power, and authority are other ways to both achieve and reflect accountability.

Accountability means that one or more parties must respond to or report to some other party or parties (Meenaghan & Washington, 1980). In professional social work, practitioners and their agencies may have to respond to professional standards or to the expectations of funders. Increasingly, this response requires some level of formal evaluation that allows subsequent reflection on the effectiveness or efficiency of agency programs. Beyond this, however, practitioners and their agencies often find that other key constituencies want to know, and even ensure, that the agencies and their practices reflect awareness of constituency expectations. In some cases accountability may stress expectations about the relevance and satisfaction of community groups and organizations (Meenaghan & Kilty, 1993). It is not that these constituencies don't care about goal achievement and effectiveness, but rather that they are more concerned about programs as symbolic statements. Specifically, a program can be a symbol that some constituency or client group is seen, noted, and judged to be significant in the eyes of an agency and its professionals.

Practitioners must be sensitive to these "extra" dimensions of practice—to the more political aspects of accountability. Clearly, practitioners can improve the formal evaluation of their practice by including affected parties as early as possible in both program design and program evaluation. Practice interventions that address problems not owned by key constituencies can fall victim to a peculiar dynamic wherein the actual effectiveness of the intervention is irrelevant to a constituency simply because the problem being addressed was never a constituency priority. This scenario can be disastrous for a practitioner and agency. The affected constituency can knowingly sabotage the intervention as a way to put the agency on notice that they want to play a role in programming.

In short, formal evaluation of practice should always reflect good practice. This means that affected parties are involved, problems are owned by constituencies, interventions are sanctioned, and the community is involved in outcome analysis. Evaluation cannot be effective when it is divorced from constituency expectations and becomes a technology owned by experts.

CONCLUSION

In this chapter we have attempted to help the practitioner understand that evaluation is an integral and integrated aspect of professional practice. It is not a burden imposed by others. The evaluative process actually guides practice. We have attempted to highlight aspects of practice evaluation by discussing issues such as the use of practice evaluation, understanding evaluation content, the setting of clear goals, establishing control groups, issues of ethical respect, and the development of pilot programs. Finally, a distinction was made between accountability and evaluation.

CHAPTER 9

Integrating Practice: A Framework for Study, Assessment, Intervention, and Follow-up

Before proceeding to the case studies, we integrate the material presented in the book. This chapter operationalizes an analytical, rational problem-solving framework for generalist practitioners working in larger systems. (The framework is an elaboration of the problem-solving worksheet in chap. 2, in light of the concepts presented in this book).

STUDY, EXPLORATION, AND DATA GATHERING

Generalist practice begins with the data gathering, or study stage. Its purpose is to give the practitioner a sense of what lies ahead. This stage, when fully operationalized for larger systems, asks the following questions.

What is the system-level problem or condition? It can be anything related to one or more of the following levels:

A group of people who live in the community: for example, inadequate after-school services

An organization or organizations that operate in the community: for example, limited access to and use of programs by certain racial or age groups; lack of appropriate interorganizational relations, producing poor networks of service, lost referrals, and so forth

A specific subcommunity or the overall community itself: for example, limited communication patterns; undeveloped group cohesion; structural and leadership processes inadequate to promote functional change

In addition to specifying the practice problem or condition by level—groups, organizations, or communities—the study stage should also determine its duration, identify consequences and affected parties, and discover who perceives the problem.

How long has the current problem been going on? This question points to possible cultural issues (norms and values) and structural issues (roles, institutional functioning, and power interests) to identify and consider, in addition to time and ongoing patterns.

Who feels the consequences of the problem? The answer should consider each of the levels—groups, organizations, and communities—as well as key individuals within each level. The consequences themselves can be specified in the following manner: *What are the negative effects at each system level and for key individuals?*

Are there associations between negative effects and specific demographic characteristics, such as race, class, gender, age, and family structure?

Are there negative effects on certain organizations in the community?

Are there negative effects on certain ethnic special interests in the community?

Are there negative effects on the community itself?

Have there been changes over time in who is negatively affected?

Consequences include positive effects. *Whose interests will be served if the problem is successfully addressed?* Again, the answer should consider level, duration, possible patterns, and changes, if any, over time.

Who perceives the problem?

Which organizations (including your own), groups, key actors, or subcommunities see the problem?

How broad is the perception?

How interested or motivated, if at all, are the identified perceivers to address the problem?

What, if anything, has been tried before to address the problem? And what have been the outcomes of these previous efforts?

Finally, *what is the nature of the problem?* Is it soft (likely to involve rearrangement of existing resources) or hard (likely to require structural change and therefore more difficult to solve)?

Perhaps the most difficult task macrolevel practitioners have is formulating clear definitions of problems to be addressed. So many problems are found in any community, neighborhood, or housing development that to take all problems on at the same time is simply impossible. Therefore, the study phase is the key to any successful plan of action. The completion of the study phase moves the process to its next logical step, a clearly formulated statement of the problem.

STATEMENT OF PROBLEM

What is the final statement of the problem to be addressed? Provide a precise rationale for considering the problem!

What situations gave rise to the problem under consideration? Give a brief summary of study phase.

What specific aspects of the problem are to be considered?

Why were these specific aspects of the problem chosen?

What ends are served by considering the identified problem?

ASSESSMENT AND STRATEGIES

In this stage the practitioner begins to map out a meaningful response to the problem that has been identified. Key to assessment is understanding power and resource patterns and fitting them to affected parties within the context of the problem as it is understood.

Relative to the organizational life of the overall community, who has power resources—by virtue of position, money, access, or investment? Is there any indication that this power pattern is present in or related to the current problem? In the context of the problem, who has power in addition to or in place of general power resources?

Who has positive power? That is, who can promote or push for change? Who has negative, or restraining, power? That is, who can or has attempted to prevent change?

What is the nature of power for each resource identified? Is it actual or merely potential power?

How slack is the use of possible resources for change?

Do the negatively affected parties—groups, organizations, and communities—have power resources? If so, what kind—actual or potential, driving or restraining?

Do the positively affected parties—groups, organizations, and communities—have power resources? If so, what kind—actual or potential, driving or restraining?

Once the range of resources has been identified and examined relative to affected parties and the problem itself, the practitioner can develop an intervention strategy that includes a range of roles for the practitioner.

DECISION AND IMPLEMENTATION

Appropriate intervention plans are related to resource patterns and take into account expected consensus or dissensus among key actors and constituencies.

If a problem is soft—that is, one that probably only requires rearrangement of resources and the purposeful use of existing skills or programs—then likely interventions include building awareness, group building, education, and preparation of planning recommendations. Appropriate corresponding practitioner roles include organizer, facilitator, staff person, group worker, enabler, and planner.

If, on the other hand, the problem is hard—that is, one that requires major changes in status or role or transfer of resources from one sector to another—then segmented support is likely; that is, some sectors might support change efforts, while others might reject it. Appropriate corresponding practitioner roles include advocate, interest advocate, and partisan activist. In short, the actual roles and derived tasks for the practitioner are based on fitting the nature of the problem to an assessment of likely resource responses.

As the practitioner prepares to move forward with the collective plan of the group—committee, task force, or board—she or he needs to take the time to once again evaluate the costs and benefits of the plan. If the costs suddenly appear to be too high, the group needs to fine-tune the decision plan. In addition, seasoned practitioners have learned that even good plans can go awry if individual group members have too many negative feelings about them. Emotions can override logic, and macropractitioners need to keep this in mind!

Finally, the practitioner needs to put one more piece of the puzzle in place before the plan is implemented and the project moves forward. It is the action element that helps to assure success by setting up what is known as "return and report." It is the accountability and responsibility piece of the project. Unless specific responsibilities are clarified and agreed upon, little happens. Therefore, the practitioner needs to introduce the following four points for discussion and consideration:

Who will be responsible for each aspect of the plan?

When will the plan be implemented, and what is the schedule for each aspect of the plan?

Where will each aspect of the plan be implemented? For example, where should we meet?

How will we actually carry out each aspect of the plan? What are our immediate, middle-range and long-range plans?

A warning note was sounded in chapter 8 about the duties and responsibilities of group members and professional practitioners. If the practitioner isn't careful, the board will assume that it is his or her responsibility to carry out all major or time-consuming aspects of the plan. Even in situations where this is possible and desirable, it nonetheless needs to be discussed because the issue of responsibility comes into play.

At each meeting of the group, all assignments are to be reported. This is how the practitioner helps to facilitate and move the project along. It is a directed, yet appropriate way of expecting and demonstrating accountability. Often one aspect of the project must be handled before the next phase can begin; return-and-report helps to keep everyone on the same page.

The last phase of the problem-solving process dictates a systematic evaluation of the project to check that the specific goals were realized and to determine the degree to which the interventions were successful or unsuccessful.

EVALUATION AND FOLLOW-UP

Successful completion of the project is not enough. Society demands greater accountability from social workers than ever before. This should not be a problem for practitioners if they have thought the whole process through thoroughly from the beginning. Evaluation is not something that can be tacked on at the end of a project. Even before a project is officially undertaken careful thought must go into the evaluation process and procedures that might be used. Seasoned macropractitioners have all experienced the frustration that comes when they suddenly realize there is no way they can fully and appropriately evaluate the effectiveness of their projects because they failed to institute certain contingencies, safeguards, or evaluative methodologies "up-front."

It is then time to look at the following five evaluation considerations:

What goals were selected?

What design was selected for collection of relevant information on program outcomes?

Who will participate in evaluation?

What role for effect? Effort? Satisfaction measures?

What change, if any, in intervention?

These five questions demonstrate the rigor and attention that must be paid to evaluation. Any time we talk about "design" and "methodology" in a process, we are indicating a requirement for exactness and a carefully conceptualized plan of action! The questions also indicate that the process demands delegation of responsibility and subsequent return-and-report.

The final step of the problem-solving framework is only complete as the practitioner follows up on the findings generated by the evaluative process. This is the feedback loop associated with systems theory. This process suggests that the practitioner and large system being served will either plan to stabilize and maintain the gain of the new program or intervention or else plan to correct the issues and problems not adequately addressed.

CONCLUSION

We have now come full circle. While very specific information and skills have been shared in this book, the premise has always been that generalist practice demands that practitioners understand and feel competent in using an analytical, rational, problem-solving process when addressing the issues of large systems. As readers integrate the content of this book in practice, the principles will come alive and take on personal meaning.

CHAPTER 10

Case Studies

We conclude with an opportunity for readers to test their understanding by applying the principles of this book in systematic critiques of three case studies developed for this purpose. These studies are real and typify the kind of challenges social work practitioners face.

Consider the *problem-solving framework* developed in chapters 2 and 9 and systematically apply that framework to the three case studies presented here. Begin by considering the *study, exploration, and data gathering* stage of case study 1. In this stage of the process identify the community of attention. For example, is Devonshire *gemeinschaft*, neogemeinschaft, or gesellschaft in its characteristics? What vertical and horizontal considerations must be taken into account? Having established these important features, determine the theoretical model and associated constructs appropriate to this specific case. For example, look at methods for assessing community type: rural method, corporate method, statistical method, social analysis method, and interactional approach (chap. 5). Remember that the model chosen will guide and help to determine the research design and the techniques employed to obtain the data needed to define the problem. Possible needs assessment strategies are field studies, community power, structure studies, community analysis, dual problems and services studies (chap. 5).

Once this initial "homework" is complete, *define the problem* to be addressed. Beware of the tendency to conceptualize problems so broadly that it's impossible to develop realistic strategies and plans of action. Imagine what it would be like to evaluate the success of a given project if the problem isn't adequately identified or articulated.

Consider ways of approaching the stated problem through carefully formulated *strategies;* for this, revisit the theoretical discussions in the book. Choice of strategy must be guided by the model most appropriate to the situation. Remember to consider the myriad of dynamics at work—formal and informal power, community beliefs and norms, communication patterns, linkages, and so forth.

There is little room for serendipity in community organization and macropractice. **You either plan for success or you have automatically planned for failure**. Remember that a large system will resist change with every fiber of its being—yes, systems are living organisms. Look at a number of possible strategies and weigh the barriers to success associated with each one. Finally, brainstorm and look very carefully at the possible consequences of the "battleplan."

At some point it's time to make a *decision* and move forward. This step is less threatening with careful planning. Understand that timing is critical. Procrastinate too much and the "window" of success may close. In addition, learn to deal with frustration—things never move as quickly or as well as we would like. Practitioners who struggle with uncertainty will have no end of problems and frustrations because there is so much in macropractice that is out of the practitioner's immediate control.

Central to ultimate success is the *implementation* of the plan. This phase of problem solving begins by identifying the model of change—social planning, locality development, social action, and so forth—that best fits the project. This choice requires a good understanding of key informants, community power brokers, community attitudes about boards and committees, and understanding and effective utilization of leadership roles, among other things. It is critical to tie down responsibility for various committee tasks. The practitioner must stay on top of assigned tasks. Remember a very important leadership principle: the quickest way in the world to alienate individual group members is to not recognize their work. Be sure to invite progress reports from all committee members who accept assignments. This simple practice assures group members that the work they do is necessary for the project to be successful.

After the project is implemented, evaluation of the effectiveness of the project should start. Don't wait for things to be well under way before developing a research design, however. Planning for evaluation must start even before the given project is a reality.

Now take the three case studies and think them through in terms of the theory and practice presented in this book. In the first two cases, we have identified some observable problems in an attempt to get readers started. In the third case readers are on their own. Obviously, none of the case studies gives all of the details needed for a "bulletproof" analysis; however, they certainly contain enough data to stimulate thought about how the scenarios might develop and what the macropractitioner's role might be.

CASE STUDY 1: DEVONSHIRE

Community Profile

Your helping agency—Yorkshire Community Service Center is a private, multipurpose agency whose function is to deal with a wide spectrum of both micro- and macroproblems. The center fosters an atmosphere of demonstration and experimentation in the delivery of services, and its professional staff and supervisors have created a climate of innovation.

The community of residence—Devonshire is a large racially mixed residential enclave near the city limits of Yorkshire. As a development it is made up almost exclusively of families with school- and preschool-age children. The average household income is approximately $30,000 per annum. Many of the women work part time and care for children, while most of the men are either blue-collar workers or clerical and sales personnel. An increasingly large number of the men—especially African American men—are unemployed. As a relatively new housing development, there is an atmosphere of social separation, with the only significant social contacts being maintained by the women. As yet, little organizational life seems to have developed in Devonshire. No churches or civic groups are housed in or near Devonshire. The only organization that exists in the Devonshire area is the public school, which was built at approximately the same time as the development. Up to this time it has been staffed exclusively by professional educators who live outside the community, and it operates only as an organization to be used by children for educational purposes. The only indigenous leadership has been exhibited by a few women and men who have served as door-to-door fundraisers for such organizations as the Heart Fund and Red Cross.

The greater community—Unlike Devonshire, Yorkshire has a rich organizational life. The city has many groups, organizations, and churches, and there has been talk of eventually constructing one or two churches directly in the Devonshire area. No one seems to be doing anything about it, however. The same apparent pattern—that is, a recognition of the need to *eventually* serve the inhabitants of Devonshire more directly—holds true for other civic and government groups and services. As a result, Devonshire residents are now forced to commute by private car out of Devonshire to Yorkshire proper for almost all services. Many lower income residents feel that this is a real hardship.

As an old community, Yorkshire has many descendants of the original inhabitants of Yorkshire—most notably the McCoys, Hatfields, and Robinsons. The McCoys have owned for many years the major downtown department store. Currently Clyde McCoy serves as the store's president, and he and his wife are heavily involved in the civic and social life of the city. Mary Hatfield has demonstrated a decided philanthropic disposition by being on the boards of directors of many agencies, including the Heart Fund, Red Cross, and Community Service Center. Clyde Hatfield is the president and founder of one of the major banks in Yorkshire. His son, a lawyer, is a promising young politician who is rumored to want to run for mayor. Ernest Robinson is the owner and operator of a light machinery plant area, which always needs employees who have some minimal training in factory work. It is located about four miles from the Devonshire area. Interestingly, his wife is the sister of Mary Hatfield, and the Hatfields and Robinsons are considered to have strong interpersonal relations. These three families along with four of five other economically prominent families are the major supporters of the local Protestant churches—especially the Presbyterian and Methodist churches.

Community and organizational factors—A handful of professional African Americans, mostly schoolteachers and social workers, live in the area of Yorkshire called Brighton. This area is contiguous to Devonshire. The remaining African Americans, mostly low-income service workers, live in the central city, very near the Yorkshire Community Service Center. Within the latter area is a group of very assertive young African Americans who are extremely disturbed about the bigotry in greater Yorkshire and who are socially separated from the African Americans who live in Brighton. While upset about the plight of African Americans in Yorkshire, however, they have had little impact on conditions in Yorkshire. Their main spokesman, Sonny James, a Baptist minister, is said to be considering a social-political campaign against the prevailing pattern of discrimination and unemployment encountered by African Americans.

Observable problems (patterned)

Isolation

Unemployment

Others

CASE STUDY 2: QUEENSBRIDGE

Community Profile

Your helping agency—Gotham Community Service Society is the oldest private social welfare agency in the city of Gotham. It has a large staff, including scores of social workers, psychologists, and consulting psychiatrists. Further, it has provided and used the services of a fairly large legal firm (Timpson and Satcher) in Gotham since the agency has a tradition of trying to create and influence social welfare policy. The agency's current director is trying to introduce a new policy of providing specific geographic areas of the city with flexible, adaptive programs and social services. The board of the agency is made up of representatives from many extremely influential city families, such as Mrs. John Gastor and Mrs. David Crockefeller. The agency has a main office in midtown Gotham and is currently contemplating opening neighborhood service centers.

The local area—Queensbridge is a section within the vast Gastoria area of Gotham. Queensbridge has about 48,000 residents, predominantly low income and nonwhite. The nonwhites (African American and Puerto Rican) have relatively large families of mainly preschool- and school-age children. Many of the families (almost 40 percent) are known to the Public Welfare Department because they qualify for income assistance and Medicaid benefits.

A major portion of Queensbridge residents live in four public housing projects that are directly adjacent to each other. Each project comprises several high-rise buildings. It is known informally in Queesbridge that Gotham funnels different groups of people into each of the four projects. Project A has a very large percentage of Puerto Rican residents. This project has the largest percentage of intact family units and is reputed to be the least crimeridden of the projects in the area. Projects B and C are inhabited mainly by large families, none of which are headed by a single parent. These projects are reputed to be dangerous because many teenagers don't regularly attend school and so roam the area. Project D is the most heterogeneous, with many elderly white widows and widowers, late-middle-age couples (mostly African American and Puerto Rican), and a good number of young mothers (African American and Puerto Rican) caring for large families.

Somewhat near the core area of Queensbridge are lower-middle- and working-class ethnic areas (Italian and Polish), where residents own their homes or live in two- or three-family houses. Most of these people are middle-aged (40s and 50s) and have fewer children than parents in the projects. Their children tend to be in their teens.

Two large public elementary schools and one large public high school serve both the core and periphery of Queensbridge. All of the schools are located several blocks from the projects, in the white lower-middle- and working-class areas of Queensbridge. Residents of these areas often complain that children from the projects yell and even periodically jostle them as the children come and go to school.

Several agencies are involved in the area because they serve particular families. They are Queens County Family Service, Gastoria Community Mental Health Center, Creedmore State Hospital (psychiatric), Gotham Public Assistance, Oakhurst General Hospital (three miles from the projects), and Gotham Child Welfare Agency. None of these agencies has an office directly in the Queensbridge section.

Queensbridge Community Development Agency, originally funded by the Office of Economic Opportunity, has been ineffective and invisible in the community. A new director, Tyrone Flynn, is attempting to revitalize the agency, but he is not sure how to use his staff, which is largely made up of case aides, most of whom live in the projects.

There are several churches in the area: one Roman Catholic, two Baptist, and two Evangelical. As yet, none has a systematized way of dealing with either the project residents or the nonproject residents. All of the clergy report shrinking revenues and membership. The housing projects all have meeting rooms in each building, but they are rarely used.

Community factors

Tyrone Flynn—Executive director of Queensbridge Community Development Agency. Former head of Gastoria Young Democrats.

Father Harry Smith—Young Catholic priest, assertive and in search of a cause. Very dissatisfied with his pastor's blindness to the problems of the area. Pastor is schoolmate of the bishop of the diocese.

Mary Virginia—Professional social worker at Oakhurst General Hospital.

Dr. R. U. Welby—Family physician practicing in Queensbridge.

Adam Dayton—African American Baptist minister, long-time political partisan on behalf of project residents. A very frustrated, yet very motivated person.

Don Carlione—Owner of Carlione's Supermarket, which serves both the projects and the neighboring ethnic areas. Well-meaning man born and raised in the area, known by everyone. Wants to keep area alive and keep his business going.

Several bar owners, beauty parlor operators, and fast-food operators who collectively have a high-volume exposure to all residents of Queensbridge.

Elected housing tenant council members in each housing project.

Several long-time project residents who are well known.

Pedro and Horace—Leaders of two large gangs, one Puerto Rican and one African American.

Staff of Gotham Community Service Society.

The greater community—Gotham is a typical large city with many neighborhoods. It is home to hundreds of corporations, local and national, and to scores of professionals and program specialists. It has a vibrant two-party system, with powerful political machines. The Democratic Party is traditionally the stronger and is currently in power. There is a strong history of good relations between the Democratic Party and the Gotham Catholic hierarchy.

Observable problems (patterned)

High isolation of housing projects

High racial/ethnic class separation within Queensbridge

Crime and perceived crime throughout Queensbridge

No medical facility in Queensbridge

Insufficient daycare for housing project residents

Apparent arbitrary and nonresponsive public housing officials

CASE STUDY 3: CENTRALIZATION OF POWER IN A LARGE POLITICAL ENTITY

In 1935 the landmark U.S. Social Security Act was signed into law, giving states across the country large amounts of federal money to administer. Also in 1935, Jane Hoey was appointed head of the U.S. Bureau of Public Assistance and began empowering strong state-level social service administrations. The consolidation of administrative power in the hands of state officials continued to build until the late 1960s, when county and local officials began to demand more input into and control of local services. In addition, America was caught in a fever of citizen participation as consumer movements, civil rights coalitions, and oppressed groups began to challenge even the state's authority. The movement had come full circle. The people were clearly demanding to be more involved and to have more say in the way money was being allocated and the way services were being delivered.

The comprehensive community mental health center movement, conceived and begun by President John F. Kennedy and implemented by the administration of Lyndon B. Johnson (1963–64), is a prominent example of this rising community fervor. The Community Mental Health Center Act (1963) mandated citizen input in both the planning and implementation phases of service delivery packages. The civil rights movement also introduced new mandates for organizing policy and advisory boards (late 1960s and early 1970s).

When local leaders and groups were given access to the decision-making process, they were surprised at the scope of decision making and the level of resources and services that had theretofore been dispensed through the state systems. In addition, local elected officials were aware that states were beginning to position themselves in ways that would assure their power to determine the delivery of social services. Many states introduced the concepts of regionalization and colocation of programs and systems.

In the early 1970s, social work delivery systems and other state agencies found themselves struggling with rapidly expanding services and contracting financial resources. As a result, they found it convenient to share with local citizen power groups decision making and, thus, funding responsibility for human service programs. Regional committees and local boards were established to coordinate the delivery of state services within a locality. Local area councils of governments were organized to coordinate different human services within a given geographic area.

Colocation, simply put, was an attempt to reduce overhead costs and to free more dollars for local direct client services. To "colocate" means literally to bring together under one roof (one building or complex) a variety of governmental and private human service agencies. Office space, receptionists, office equipment, furniture, and other resources are shared. Such an arrangement can benefit clients because they are subjected to less "red tape" and receive multiple services from different state agencies without having to leave the building or immediate grounds. Colocation only enjoyed moderate success as an organizing concept for a variety of reasons that will be discussed later in this case study.

There had always been natural tension between various governing bodies. States had always been suspicious of the power and control wielded by the federal government, but suddenly they found themselves the target of local governments and consumer groups. They were challenged constantly by local grassroot movements that wanted more say in the way services were delivered.

In 1974, a politically conservative, largely rural state began to toy with the idea of unifying a variety of individually strong, state-centralized public entitlement programs: health services, corrections, social services, and educational programs (including vocational rehabilitation) into one state-level unified department. This move to pull the authority and control of human service programs back into a single state-level department was proposed as a way to break the power of individual service boards and combine members into one large advisory board, for all social and human services. The unification movement, which was to be organized into regional administrative units, flew in the face of the national trend of the times. Major local service agency directors broke into a "cold sweat" at the mere suggestion of such a reorganization. Issues of program autonomy, scarce resources, altruism, and overall fear of the capriciousness so often associated with large bureaucratic entities quickly became the focus of discussion throughout the state.

In an attempt to head off the proposed unification—and suspected state takeover—a group of agency directors in a semirural county approached a fellow social worker to chair what was to be known as the Human Resource Task Force. The licensed social worker selected to chair the task force was well acquainted with the professional and political tenor of the community because he had worked at the area's state mental hospital and was one of the founders of the local comprehensive mental health center. More important, as a professor at a local university, he was not viewed as having a conflict of interest, because he was not formally affiliated with any of the funding agencies associated with the task force.

Because of the rural nature of the state, agency directors had been beset by criticism from their constituencies, especially in more isolated areas, about the inaccessibility of services. Local citizens were irate at having to travel significant distances to receive any kind of service.

The task force determined that by establishing their own regionalized, colocated services the local agencies could counter the state's move toward unification and offer the people of the state an alternative to the mass state-level reorganization being proposed. They thought that through mutual cooperation they could, in fact, offer better client services and yet provide substantial cost savings to the residents of the state.

It was decided by the Human Resource Task Force that they would establish a Human Services Center in the largest farm community near many of the complaining citizens. A major consideration in the selection of the community was the town's mayor and his support for the project. The mayor shared the vision of services that could be made available to his constituency and thus jumped at the opportunity to be involved. His decision to become involved with the task force, and to help to pilot the project, would be either a political disaster or a real political coup. The mayor's support was not empty words. Rather, his commitment translated into the remodeling of the city library basement as the home for the center. As a result of his efforts, a major investment for the small community, the library became the newest public building in town and the hub of community activity.

The agencies that originally came together in this cooperative pilot project were the state Department of Child and Family Services (DCFS), the local comprehensive mental health center, a community action agency from the county seat, adult probation and parole services, and a church-sponsored adoption, foster care, and clinical counseling program. These agencies were to later be joined by social security and state vocational rehabilitation services.

The task force decided to begin the Human Service Center with one generalist social worker and a full-time secretary. The social worker would conduct the initial interview of all new clients and then make appropriate referrals to part-time professionals in the other participating agencies. Each of the agencies would have regularly scheduled hours in the facility for their staff so that the center's secretary could arrange their client appointments. The agencies would then send whatever number of workers they needed to meet the client demands for the day. Each agency would have the option of moving clients from the central office to the colocated facility.

The chair of the task force immediately confronted the problem of how to fund the new center. As might be anticipated, the hiring of two full-time workers, who officially represented no particular agency, became a fiscal and administrative challenge. As a result, the chair and representatives of the major agencies involved requested a meeting with the governor's community affairs assistant to secure state support for the pilot project and to seek financial support for the initial staff positions.

The community affairs assistant was initially somewhat cool with the task force representatives because he had been warned that "a group of angry, rabble-rousers were seeking his ear." However, after the project was carefully laid out, the tension eased and a cooperative effort supported by the governor's office enabled the task force to receive federal and state Community Education and Training Act (CETA) funds through the local council of governments (COG) office and a group of local mayors. A formal program grant with carefully articulated objectives and a proposed budget, was submitted to the COG that December (1974). With COG approval all components were in place to officially launch the project. In the fall of 1975 the center had its official opening.

The task force members returned to the capitol after the first year of operation. On this occasion they were invited to meet with the governor who expressed considerable pleasure with the success of the center. More important, he was so impressed with the cooperative efforts of the agencies, the community leaders, and the private sector that he offered to find state funding so that the pilot period could be extended and so that a formal evaluation process could be put in place.

How many potential or actual macrolevel practice problems or issues can you identify in this case study? How and what might you do about these issues to resolve them?

Some more obvious issues suggested by the case study are viewing organizations as "corporate actors" (kingdom building); identifying communities (gemeinschaft vs. gesellschaft); resolving power struggles (formal vs. informal); dealing with turf protection issues of participating agencies; putting aside petty agency jealousies; addressing the (client) "participation paradox"; choosing level of autonomy (administrative control); enforcing confidentiality (computers and the master service unit); understanding agency directors' vulnerable positions as they "bite the hand that feeds them"; sharing governance; assigning fiscal authority; overcoming resistance to change and fear of bureaucracies; organizing, and coalitions; committees; grant writing; evaluating programs; applying professional values (taking a responsible position rather than just whining about unification); providing leadership; viewing organizations in environments; managing small group dynamics; understanding community politics; assigning responsibility for a mongrel agency (who does the axe fall on if things go awry?); and weighing political strategy (the federal/state/local paradox).

While the colocation efforts proved very successful and won the accolades of the governor, the director of the state Department of Human Services continued with the plans for unification and reorganization. The director obviously had his own political agenda, and it appeared that nothing was going to deter him from completing his mission. While the director of human services knew of the Human Resource Task Force he was not particularly alarmed about it, regarding it as no real threat to his unification plan. In fact, it had been reported that he was amused by the whole notion. The director was reported to have said, "Those local social service agency directors will never be able to cooperate and work together." Clearly, he was counting on turf issues to sabotage all cooperative efforts.

In 1978, the director of the Department of Human Services stepped up his unification implementation plans by naming a steering committee that would look at consolidation and colocation issues for all units and divisions within his department. In response, the county commissioners in some semirural areas raised questions about the impact of the new mandate coming from the capitol.

Because of their mutual nervousness about state control, local COGs and county commissioners from three adjacent counties came together to form a larger regionally incorporated Tri-County Association of Governments (TAG) to consider how to solve their dilemma. The local social worker who had chaired the Human Resource Task Force was invited to chair a new TAG committee of community leaders, who would be named by the county commissioners. The selection strategy was to keep the committee in the legislative political arena and out of the hands of executive state-level human and social service agency employees. The composition of this committee was critical to any success that might be achieved, but unfortunately, the chair had no input in the composition and selection of the committee members except for their number. A variety of educators, prominent business owners, homemakers, and political figures were initially selected. The TAG demonstrated its commitment to the success of the committee by assigning its own paid executive director and his personal secretary to provide 25 percent of their time to the efforts of the committee.

The initial work of the committee was very emotional and tedious largely because of one strong, verbal member of the committee. Little or no progress was made for almost three meetings (one and a half months) because of his resistance and disruption. A former state legislator, he stonewalled the group process because he was uncertain about the "real" purpose of the committee and as a result didn't want to get "set up" and known as a "political puppet." He knew that the major issue was political, and he didn't want to waste his time developing recommendations that would be ignored. Or even worse, he didn't want to become a "rubber stamp" for the county commissioners and mayors. He, more than the others, knew that local politicians felt they faced a dilemma: they didn't want to be responsible for social service programs, but they also didn't want the state imposing programs on them. Finally, he knew that the whole issue would ultimately crystalize into a power struggle among the federal, state, and local authorities.

The tenor of the committee's work began to change after the executive director of the TAG came to the third meeting and issued a clear, specific charge. He reaffirmed that he and his secretary would be available at all meetings and would assist in all the "leg work" needed to make the committee successful. He also assured the committee that all discussions would be confidential and that nothing would be released or discussed without the committee's prior approval.

The committee's work was interrupted once more when the TAG executive director's assistant tried an "end run" and made an unapproved recommendation supportive of unification to the state human service authorities. It was later learned that the TAG employee was a friend of the state human service director and was trying to secure for himself a more prestigious position with the state. This unprecedented move ultimately cost the individual his job. Fortunately, the employee was not aware of all the committee's work and as a result did not "tip the hand" of the committee. Indeed, the experience confirmed the confidentiality with which the executive director was managing his office; the dismissed TAG employee had little knowledge of the committee's real agenda.

The TAG committee began a very careful, methodical year-long review of the many issues and implications of the state's proposed unification project. It began its factfinding by inviting each administrator (usually the director) of the many units to be involved in the state's proposed reorganization project to a three- to four-hour meeting in order to discuss and answer a specific set of questions developed by the committee. The volume of information thus generated was considerable because each unit had its own specific set of concerns unique to the work in which it engaged.

Some common themes led to the final recommendations made by the TAG committee: the governor's ownership of the drive to consolidate services; the governor's understanding of the number of major departments, as well as divisions, being unified into one large, perhaps cumbersome entity; the governor's awareness of the significance of the power shift being suggested and the governor's intent to centralize this much power under one department head; the apparent contradiction between the state unification of services and federal decentralization of services (local authority); and the local COGs' and regional area councils of government's (ACOGs) lack of adequate information on which to make reasoned decisions and act on behalf of their constituencies. ACOGs were composed of mayors and commissioners from adjoining counties who came together in either area or regional associations of government; TAG was an example of a regional association. Once each year all of the state's COGs and ACOGs joined together in a weeklong retreat. The mayors and county commissioners used this time to share notes and strategize for more local control. The rural leaders also used this time to coalesce and "flex their muscles" against the urban COGs.

As each unit was interviewed it became apparent that information was being heavily manipulated at the state level. Not only were minor details of the reorganization being withheld, but critical concepts were not being shared or discussed. For example, the COGs and ACOGs were being told that they would be active participating members in the delivery of services under unification because they would be included on local boards. Only later did the TAG committee learn that those boards would be advisory and not policy-setting entities. This discovery was particularly infuriating to local elected officials because they felt they had been misled. It was also an especially sensitive issue because so many discretionary federal funds were flowing into the state and local authorities wanted to have stronger (certainly not weaker) influence on the distribution and use of those funds.

After all the meetings were conducted and the data compiled, the TAG factfinding committee made two presentations to the TAG leadership in order to obtain their input and to seek further direction. This became a tricky task when the local TAG leaders became incensed at what they perceived to be a state power grab. TAG officials had difficulty understanding that neither they nor the committee should do anything precipitous because the state still held all the cards, meaning that the dollars must flow *through the state* to the local governmental units. TAG members came away from these two meetings feeling a great deal of frustration with the state of affairs but also pride and ownership in the work their committee was doing. They agreed to be discrete and to keep the work of the committee confidential.

These policymakers then invited the committee to identify three of four organizational designs for them to consider. Ultimately, four workable alternatives were developed, and the potential strengths and weaknesses of each design were carefully identified and articulated. The TAG leadership reviewed the committee's recommendations and chose the option they thought best served their constituency.

The TAG committee prepared to present its work to the state senate subcommittee responsible for reviewing the Department of Human Service's unification implementation proposal. The senate's calendar was followed very carefully, and when the unification proposal came up for review, the TAG committee sought an opportunity to present the TAG's position on the matter.

The appearance of the TAG committee members and a few key TAG elected officials caught the administrators of the Department of Human Services completely by surprise. These administrators were not prepared to respond to the committee's report. Even more devastating to their plan, the TAG committee presented a written document stating that all the COGs and ACOGs in the entire state had met and were endorsing the TAG proposal, officially opposing the state's concept of unification. The TAG committee then stressed that both national and state trends were to move toward greater regionalization and local involvement, responsibility, and authority. The committee demonstrated the irony in the state's request for local service unification under even greater central state control at a time when elected legislators were on record as supporting more local and regional control of programs. Out of exasperation, a state administrator of human services said, "What the TAG is proposing is not unification." To which a member of the audience replied, "There never was a state mandate for unification." Finally, the TAG chair brought the committee's report to a close by saying, "Let's then say we are proposing an alternate plan for the delivery of social service." Unification was officially dead!

Epilogue—Unfortunately, as the meeting ended an elderly county commissioner, who had an ongoing feud with the state over forest lands and who had also been quite suspicious of the TAG committee, stood up and shouted, "We've beat them. We've finally won. We got 'em today." As a result, the state administrators left the senate chambers very angry. The elderly commissioner, with his own agenda, didn't understand the political wisdom that when you appear to have won a particular battle you don't corner and embarrass your opponents. He didn't understand the value of permitting people to retreat with dignity and of keeping the focus on issues and not personalities.

How many potential or actual macrolevel practice problems or issues can you identify in this part of the case study? How and what might you do about these issues to resolve them? What problem-solving technique would you use?

Some of the more obvious issues suggested by the second part of the case study are understanding individual versus structural effects; countering personal ambition; knowing the enemy, or "doing your homework;" managing communication; working quietly and keeping the opposition in the dark; carefully timing all public announcements and appearances; understanding the ground rules; being realistic about who has the upper hand at any given time; avoiding the bluff (it isn't a card game); understanding that you can win a battle and still lose the war; understanding the power of coalitions; understanding what win-win really means; understanding the power of compromise and consensus (being certain of the gains and losses); viewing organizations as "corporate actors" and knowing what it takes to be successful with them; mastering the "logic of collective action"; role taking versus role making; ensuring performance (service vs. procedures, etc.); providing leadership; avoiding default and fragmented accountability; designing and enforcing the "rules of the game"; countering relative deprivation and the "revolution of rising entitlements"; reframing conflict; negotiating (let's talk vs. the end justifies the means); evaluating bureaucratic versus professional contexts; and achieving organization versus "fate" (a matter of degree).

BIBLIOGRAPHY

Allen-Meares, P., Washington, R. O., & Welsh, B. L. (2000). *Social work services in schools* (3rd ed.). Boston: Allyn and Bacon.

Anderson, J. (1997). *Social work with groups: A process model.* New York: Longman.

Anderson, J. D. (1982, Fall). Generic and generalist practice and the BSW curriculum. *Journal of Education for Social Work, 18*(3), 37–45.

Anderson, R. E., & Carter, I. E. (1977). *Human behavior in the social environment: A social systems approach.* Chicago: Aldine.

Anderson, R. E., & Carter, I. (1990). *Human behavior in the social environment.* Chicago: Aldine.

Arches, J. (1991). Social structure, burnout and job satisfaction. *Social Work, 36,* 202–206.

Arendt, H. (1959). *The human condition.* Garden City, NY: Doubleday.

Austin, D. R. (1982). *Therapeutic recreation processes and techniques.* New York: Wiley.

Barker, R. L. (1995). *The social work dictionary* (3rd ed.). Washington, DC: NASW Press.

Barnard, C. (1948). *Function of executives.* Cambridge, MA: Harvard University Press.

Beal, G. M., Bohlen, J. M., & Raudabaugh, J. N. (1962). *Leadership and dynamic group action.* Ames: Iowa State University Press.

Beebe, L., Winchester, N. A., Edwards, R. L., et al. (Eds.). (1995). *Encyclopedia of social work, 2* (19th ed.). Washington, DC: NASW Press.

Bennis, W. G., Benne, K. D., & Chin, R. (1969). *The planning of change* (2nd ed.). New York: Holt, Rinehart, and Winston.

Berger, P. L. & Luckman, T. (1966). *The social construction of reality.* Garden City, NY: Anchor.

Biddle, B. J., & Thomas, E. J. (Eds.). (1966). *Role theory: Concepts and research.* New York: John Wiley & Sons.

Bilken, D. P. (1983). *Community organizing: Theory and practice.* Englewood Cliffs, NJ: Prentice-Hall.

Billsberry, J. (Ed.). (1996). *The effective manager: Perspectives and illustrations.* London: Sage.

Blau, P. M., & Marshall, M. W. (1971). *Bureaucracy in modern society.* New York: Random House.

Bloom, M., & Fisher, J. (1982). *Evaluation practice: Guidelines for the accountable professional.* Englewood Cliffs, NJ: Prentice-Hall.

Brandwein, R. (1978). *Utilization of formal service networks by female headed families: From passive recipient to active participant.* Iowa City: University of Iowa School of Social Work.

Brandwein, R. (1987). Women and community organization. In D. S. Burden & N. Gottlieb et al. (Eds.), *The woman client: Providing human services in a changing world.* (pp. 111–125). New York: Tavisock/Routledge.

Breton, M. (1994). Relating competence promotion and empowerment. *Journal of Progressive Human Services, 5*(1), 27–44.

Brueggemann, W. G. (1996). *The practice of macro social work.* Chicago: Nelson-Hall.

Cartwright, D., & Zander, A. (Eds.). (1968). *Group dynamics* (3rd ed.). New York: Harper & Row.

Castex, G. M. (1994). Providing services to Hispanic/Latino populations: Profiles in diversity. *Social Work, 39,* 288–295.

Chow, J., & Coulton, C. (1996). Strategic use of community data base for planning and practice. *Computers in Human Services, 13*(3), PPP–PPP.

Clift, R. T., et al. (1995). *Collaborative leadership and shared decision making.* New York: Teachers College Press.

Compton, B., & Galaway, B. (1999). *Social work processes* (6th ed.). Pacific Grove, CA: Brooks Cole.

Coser, L. A. (1967). *Continuities in the study of social conflict.* New York: Free Press.

Council on Social Work Education. Commission on accreditation. (1994). *Handbook of accreditation standards and procedures* (4th ed.). Alexandria, VA: Author.

Cox, F. M., Erlich, J. L., Rothman, J., & Tropman, J. E. (Eds.). (1979). *Strategies of community organization* (3rd ed.). Itasca, IL: F. E. Peacock.

Cox, F. M., Erlich, J. L., Rothman, J., & Tropman, J. E. (Eds.). (1987). *Macro practice: Strategies of community organization* (4th ed.). Itasca, IL: F. E. Peacock.

Dahl, R. A. (1962). *Who governs? Democracy and power in an American city.* New Haven, CT: Yale University Press.

DiNitto, D. M. & McNeece, C. A. (1995). *Social work: issues and opportunities in a challenging profession.* Needham Heights, MA: Allyn and Bacon.

DuBois, B., & Miley, K. K. (1999). *Social work: An empowering profession.* Boston: Allyn and Bacon.

Duke, J. T. (1976). *Conflict and power in social life.* Provo, UT: Brigham Young University Press.

Dunham, A. (1958). *Community welfare organization: Principles and practice.* New York: Thomas Y. Crowell.

Ecklein, J. (1984). *Community organizers* (2nd ed.). New York: John Wiley & Sons.

Fellin, P. (1987). *The community and the social worker.* Itasca, IL: F. E. Peacock.

Fellin, P. (1995). *The community and the social worker.* Itasca, IL: F. E. Peacock.

French, J., & Raven, B. (1968). The basis of social power. In D. Cartwright (Ed.), *Studies in social power.* Ann Arbor: University of Michigan Press.

Germain, C. B., & Gitterman, A. (1996). *The life model of social work practice: Advances in theory and practice.* New York: Columbia University Press.

Giddens, A. (1984). *The constitution of society.* San Francisco: University of California Press at Berkeley.

Greenleaf, R. K. (1977). *Servant leadership: A journey into the nature of legitimate power and greatness.* Mahwah, NJ: Paulist Press.

Grosser, C. F. (1976). *New directions in community organization: From enabling to advocacy* (Expanded ed.). New York: Praeger.

Guilford, J. P. (1966). Intelligence: 1965 model. *American Psychologist, 21*(1), 20–26.

Hardcastle, D. A., Wenocur, S., & Powers, P. R. (1997). *Community practice: Theories and skills for social workers.* New York: Oxford University Press.

Hardin, G. (1968). The tragedy of the commons. *Science, 162,* 1243–1248.

Hill, W. F. (1971). *Learning: A survey of psychological interpretations* (Rev. ed.). Scranton, PA: Chandler.

Hunter, F. (1953). *Community power structure: A study of decision makers.* Chapel Hill: University of North Carolina Press.

Johnson, D. W., & Johnson, F. P. (1994). *Joining together: Group theory and group skills.* Englewood Cliffs, NJ: Prentice-Hall.

Johnson, L. C. (1998). *Social work practice: A generalist approach* (6th ed.). Boston: Allyn and Bacon.

Karger, H. J., & Fisher, R. (1997). *Social work and community in a private world: Getting out in public.* White Plains, NY: Longman.

Kirst-Ashman, K. K., & Hull, G., Jr. (1997A). *Understanding generalist practice* (2nd ed.). Chicago: Nelson-Hall.

Kirst-Ashman, K. K., & Hull, G. H., Jr. (1997B). *Generalist practice with organizations and communities.* Chicago: Nelson-Hall.

Konopka, G. (1972). *Social group work: A helping process* (2nd ed.). Englewood Cliffs, NJ: Prentice-Hall.

Kramer, R. M., & Specht, H. (Eds.). (1975). *Readings in community organization practice* (2nd ed.). Englewood Cliffs, NJ: Prentice-Hall.

Kramer, R. M., & Specht, H. (Eds.). (1983). *Readings in community organization practice* (3rd ed.). Englewood Cliffs, NJ: Prentice-Hall.

Landon, P. S. (1995). Generalist and advanced generalist practice. In L. Beebe, N. A. Winchester, R. L. Edwards, et al. (Eds.), *Encyclopedia of social work* (pp. 1101–1107). Washington, DC: NASW Press.

LaPiere, R. T. (1965). *Social change.* New York: McGraw-Hill.

Lewin, K. (1952). Group decision and social madness. In G. E. Swanson, T. N. Nowcomb, & E. L. Hartley (Eds.), *Readings in social psychology.* New York: Holt, Rinehart, and Winston.

Lewin, K. H., Lippett, R., & White, R. K. (1939). Patterns of aggressive behavior in experimentally created social climates. *Journal of Social Psychology, 10,* 271–299.

Mayer, R. (1972). *Social planning and social change.* Englewood Cliffs, NJ: Prentice-Hall.

McGregor, D. (1960). *The human side of enterprise.* New York: McGraw-Hill.

McMahon, M. O. (1994). *Advanced generalist practice with an international perspective.* Englewood Cliffs, NJ: Prentice-Hall.

Meenaghan, T. M., & Kilty, K. M. (1993). *Policy analysis and research technology: Political and ethical considerations.* Chicago: Lyceum Books.

Meenaghan, T. M., Powers, G. T., & Toomey, B. G. (1985). *Practice focused research: Integrating human service practice and research.* Englewood Cliffs, NJ: Prentice-Hall.

Meenaghan, T. M., & Washington, R. (1980). *Social policy and social welfare: Structure and applications.* New York: Free Press.

Meenaghan, T. M., Washington, R. O., & Ryan, R. M. (1982). *Macro practice in the human services: An introduction to planning, administration, evaluation, and community organizing components of practice.* New York: Free Press.

Miley, K. K., O'Melia, M., & Dubois, B. L. (1998). *Generalist social work practice: An empowering approach* (2nd ed.). Needham Heights, MA: Allyn and Bacon.

Miringoff, M. L. (1980). *Management in human service organizations.* New York, Macmillan.

Morgan, G. (1997). *Images of organization* (2nd ed.). Thousand Oaks, CA: Sage.

Morris, V. C. (1961). *Philosophy and the American school.* Boston: Houghton Mifflin.

Netting, F. E., Kettner, P. M., & McMurtry, S. L. (1993). *Social work macro practice.* New York: Longman.

Olson, M., Jr. (1965). *Logic of collective action.* Cambridge, MA: Harvard University Press.

Parsons, T. (1951). *The social system.* Glencoe, IL: Free Press.

Perlman, R., & Gurin, A. (1972). *Community organization and social planning.* New York: John Wiley & Sons.

Peter, L. J. & Hull, R. (1996). The peter principle. In J. Billsberry et al. (Eds.), *The effective manager: Perspectives and illustrations.* (pp. 209–213). London: Sage Publications.

Pincus, A., & Minahan, A. (1973). *Social work practice: Model and method.* Itasca, IL: F. E. Peacock.

Quinn, J. B. (1980). *Strategies for change: Logical incrementalism.* Homewood, IL: Richard D. Irwin.

Rapp, C. A., & Poertner, J. (1992). *Social administration: A client-centered approach.* New York: Longman.

Raven, B., & Kruglanski, A. (1970). Conflict and power. In P. Swingle (Ed.), *The structure of conflict.* New York: Academic Press.

Rivera, F. G., & Erlich, J. L. (1981). Neo-gemeinschaft minority communities: Implications for community organization in the United States. *Community Development Journal, 18*(3), 189–200.

Rothman, J. (1996). The interweaving of community intervention approaches with personal preface by the author. *Journal of Community Practice: Organizing, Planning, Development and Change, 3*(3/4).

Rothman, J., Erlich, J. L., & Tropman, J. E. (Eds.). (1995). *Strategies of community intervention* (5th ed.). Itasca, IL: F. E. Peacock.

Rubin, A., & Babbie, E. (1997). *Research Methods for Social Work* (3rd ed.). Belmont: Brooks-Cole.

Rubin, H. J., & Rubin, I. (1986). *Community organizing and development.* Columbus, OH: Merrill.

Schein, E. H. (1985). *Organizational culture and leadership.* San Francisco: Jossey-Bass.

Selltiz, C., Jahoda, M., Deutsch, M., & Cook, S. W. (1959). *Research methods in social relations* (Rev. ed.). New York: Holt, Rinehart, and Winston.

Shafritz, J. M., & Ott, J. S. (1987). *Classics of organization theory* (2nd ed.). Chicago: Dorsey.

Shatz, M. S., Jenkins, L. E., & Sheafor, B. W. (1990, Fall). Milford redefined: A model of initial and advanced generalist social work. *Journal of Social Work Education, 26,* 217–231.

Sheafor, B. W., Horejsi, C. R., & Horejsi, G. A. (2000). *Techniques and guidelines for social work practice* (5th ed.). Boston: Allyn and Bacon.

Skidmore, R. A. (1995). *Social work administration: Dynamic management and human relationships* (3rd ed.). Boston: Allyn and Bacon.

Tolson, E. R., Reid, W. J., & Garvin, C. D. (1994). *Generalist practice: A task-centered approach.* New York: Columbia University Press.

Tripodi, T. (1983). *Evaluative research for social workers.* Englewood Cliffs, NJ: Prentice-Hall.

Tropman, J. E., Erlich, J. L., & Rothman, J. (Eds.). (1995). *Tactics and techniques of community intervention* (3rd ed.). Itasca, IL: F. E. Peacock.

Warren, R. L. (1978). *The community in America* (3rd ed.). Chicago: Rand McNally.

Weber, M. (1947). *Theory of social and economic organization* (A. Henderson & T. Parsons, Trans.). Glencoe, IL: Free Press.

Weil, M. (Ed.). (1996). Model development in community practice: An historical perspective. *Journal of Community Practice: Organizing, Planning, Development and Change, 3*(3/4).

Wells, C. C. (1989). *Social work day to day: The experience of generalist social work practice* (2nd ed.). White Plains, NY: Longman.

Williams, R. M. Jr. (1951). *American society.* New York: Alfred A. Knopf.

INDEX